What people are say

"The apostle John wrote, 'I have no greater joy than to hear that my children are walking in truth' (3 John 4). My sentiments exactly! Reading *Limitless* has been a source of great joy to a father's heart. Its pages abound in God's timeless, life-changing truth that is too often overlooked or taken for granted. What a thrill to hear how our Lord can marvelously take His living truth and transfer it from the head to the heart—only a distance of fourteen inches, but definitely the trip of a lifetime! May all of us be encouraged to join you, Ben! We all need this reminder to climb back into the arms of God's limitless love and grace— right where we belong. Thanks for sharing your dynamic journey with Jesus. I know I needed it!"

— Tim Dailey, DMin, senior pastor, Life Connection Church, Kuwait

"Many people live life *striving* in their own efforts rather than *thriving* in God's grace. Ben Dailey candidly tells his story of discovering and embracing one of God's greatest gifts. If you allow it, this message will transform the way you look at the grace of God and empower you to live a free and full life."

— John Bevere, author of multiple bestselling books; minister and founder of Messenger International

"One of the words Ben Dailey uses in his book to describe the way many Christians live is *grind*. That's so very true and so very sad. When we aren't thrilled with the treasure that is Jesus, we're left with our own attempts to earn approval. But no matter how much we do, it's never enough. Life becomes an unceasing grind, and our hearts are plugged shut. We hear about love, but we don't feel loved. We read about joy, but we feel discouraged or arrogant. Ben shows us another way, the way God intended all along: accepting His wonderful gift of grace and letting it change us from the inside out."

— Tommy Barnett, senior pastor, Phoenix First Assembly; founder of the Los Angeles Dream Center

"Ben Dailey hits the nail on the head—he obliterates our addiction to performance and achievement by reminding us about the amazing nature of God's grace! This book is liberating, but it will probably make legalists as mad as hornets. If you've been bound by religion or crave the freedom that comes from Jesus Christ, then Ben's book is a good first step toward a renewed faith in a limitless God and an unleashed life."

— Dr. David Anderson, author of *Gracism*

"We aren't defined by what we do for God, but rather, by what God already did for us. In *Limitless*, Ben Dailey takes us on a journey that will correct spiritual and religious myopia so we can embrace the catalytic message of Christ-rendered grace—a grace that is sufficient indeed!"

— Dr. Samuel Rodriguez, president of NHCLC/CONELA, Hispanic Evangelical Association; general bishop, Pentecostal Church of God

"Many writers communicate factual information, but a few give voice to a life-changing encounter they're experiencing. In *Limitless*, Ben Dailey invites us to go on a journey to discover what has transformed his life and ministry: the incredible and empowering grace of God. *Limitless* isn't just good advice on how to live, nor is it a set of principles of self-improvement that promise more success in life. Rather, it's the announcement of an entirely new way of living—the empowerment of grace that's found in the person of Jesus Christ. Read it expectantly, and you'll discover that you can be a person of unlimited possibilities!"

— Bishop Tony Miller, The Gate Church, Oklahoma City, Oklahoma

"All books seek to communicate content, but few deliver the candor necessary to engage the reader in a 'me too' experience. My friend Ben Dailey's book, *Limitless,* brings rich content wrapped in vulnerable candor. From the very first page, you'll say 'me too.' Get ready to embrace your *limitless* life!"

— Dr. Sam Chand, leadership consultant and author of *Leadership Pain,* (www.samchand.com)

"*Stunning.* That's the word that comes to mind when I read Ben's book, *Limitless.* He articulately and boldly describes the wonder of God's grace, but he also describes the difficulty of embracing it. Why do we resist grace? Because we want to prove ourselves to God and to others. God save us from our foolish pride! Ben, thank you for pointing us to the life-changing grace, love, and mercy of God."

—Benny Perez, pastor, The Church, Las Vegas, Nevada

"Pastor Ben Dailey's book *Limitless* is amazing! I love the way he uses his personal journey to drive home wonderful truths. More than just theories, these heartwarming biblical insights have been proven in the laboratory of life at Calvary Church in Irving, Texas. Read this book and you will learn how Ben moved from feeling like a failure to finding the life he was always meant to live. And as you read it, you'll find the life you were meant to live too."

— Michael Pitts, founder and bishop, Cornerstone Church, Toledo, Ohio

"Grace. We desperately need it, but we often resist it. Instead, we get on a treadmill of self-effort, but no matter how much we do to prove ourselves, we still feel empty, exhausted, and confused. In *Limitless*, Ben Dailey shows us the insanity of staying on the treadmill when Jesus offers us His love, a new identity, and genuine spiritual power. This book will get you off the treadmill so you can live the abundant life God intended you to live!"

— Herbert Cooper, senior pastor, People's Church, Oklahoma City, Oklahoma; author of *But God Changes Everything*

"In his book *Limitless*, Ben Dailey performs open-heart surgery on all of us, revealing how even a devout and committed follower of Christ can be drawn into the circle of guilt for never being 'good enough.' Ben helps us regain the fresh perspective of grace we all felt when our salvation was new."

— Bil Cornelius, founding pastor, Church Unlimited, Corpus Christi, Texas; bestselling author of *Today Is the Day*

"One of the greatest challenges we will ever face in life is the constant, unrelenting, internal drive to measure up. It's the bone-jarring reality that no matter how full our lives, businesses, and ministries are, we continually grapple with a sense of emptiness. From the deep well of personal experience, Ben Dailey offers us hope in knowing that this is far from God's plan for our lives. Ben introduces us to the kind of grace that's truly sufficient. As you turn each page, prepare to be equipped with tools straight from heaven that will enable you to walk in grace and live in joy. Are you tired of the struggle? Read this book and get ready to be equipped to strangle the struggle through the unyielding, limitless love of Jesus!"

— Jim Raley, pastor, Calvary Christian Center, Ormond Beach, Florida

"To prejudge everyone and everything through the person and work of Jesus Christ—that is the creed of what I call a 'gracist.' Ben Dailey qualifies as a radical person of grace. His blunt honesty in *Limitless* is both delightful and demanded. Like Ben, many of us who have grown up in the church have been bewitched to believe another gospel. A gospel that began in grace but drifted into an I-will-work-for-salvation deception. The bait and switch of religion has caused many to cut the line of their faith. Someone please take us back to the cross. Help us to stare at the sacrificial work of Christ until we vow never again to insult grace with our works of the flesh. Ben Dailey has taken on that task, and you are the fortunate beneficiary of this timely and needed message. Tap the limitless power of grace."

— Phil Munsey, chairman, Champion Network of Churches with Joel Osteen Ministries

"Every biblical theme is extremely important but not equally consequential. For example, eschatology is an important subject, but our lives aren't adversely affected if we don't completely understand it. Grace, on the other hand, is one of the subjects that we cannot afford to misunderstand. In his book, *Limitless*, my good friend Ben Dailey does a masterful job of reintroducing us to this vital truth. His information is enlightening, his candor is inspiring, and his humility is refreshing. In this book, Ben takes you on a journey that has the potential to change your life. Your limits have an expiration date: they come off when you read this material. Get ready for a limitless life."

— Dharius Daniels, pastor, Kingdom Church, Ewing, New Jersey; author of *RePresent Jesus*

"I'm honored to read the revelation of Ben Dailey as he unfolds the limitless grace of Jesus Christ. But the real honor for me is that I've been privileged to witness the limitless grace of Jesus Christ expressed in Ben's life. I've seen limitless love as he pastors his church, ministers to people, leads staff, and completes the tasks of ministry. But that's not all. I've seen limitless grace in Ben's life beyond this: I see limitless love as a father, husband, brother, friend, man, and person. Thank you, Ben, for showing us how limitless God's love is, not just in the pages of this book, but also in the pages of your life."

— Charles Scott, general bishop, Pentecostal Church of God

BEN DAILEY

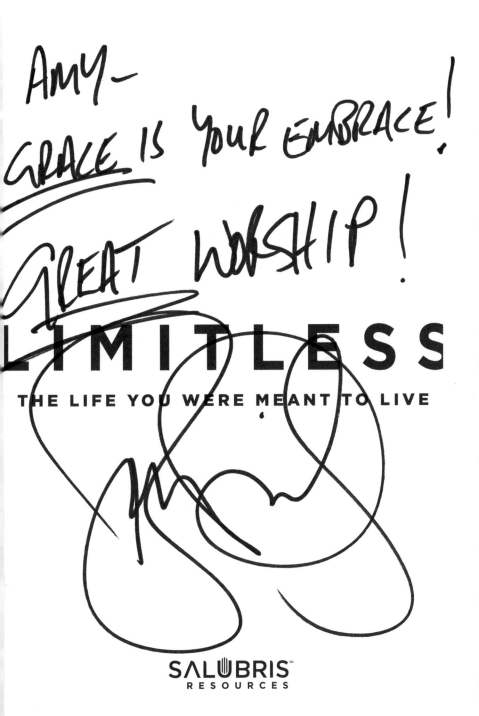

AMY —
GRACE IS YOUR EMBRACE!
GREAT WORSHIP!

LIMITLESS

THE LIFE YOU WERE MEANT TO LIVE

SALUBRIS
RESOURCES

Published by Salubris Resources
1445 N. Boonville Ave.
Springfield, Missouri 65802
www.salubrisresources.com

Cover design by PlainJoe Studios (www.plainjoestudios.com)
Interior formatting by Anne McLaughlin

ISBN: 978-1-68067-112-4

19 18 17 16 • 1 2 3 4 5

Printed in the United States of America

To Kim.

I spent much of my life searching for a treasure,

but I didn't realize the treasure God had already given me in you.

You are a gift from the hand of God, a true picture of His grace to me.

CONTENTS

FOREWORD

I met Ben Dailey more than twenty-two years ago when he was a first-year student in Bible college. Even before we spoke to one another, I sensed a divine connection between his spirit and mine. Instantly, I wanted to know him "up close and personal."

Days later when we were together again, God gave me a precise directive regarding my future relationship with Ben. I knew, without question, that I was to be connected with him in ministry. God said to me, "Open the door and make room for Ben in your life." Amazingly, this directive from God came to me before I had spoken a single word to Ben.

Soon, Ben and I talked and began to make preliminary plans for a ministry partnership. At the time, I had no knowledge of either the depth or length of what our relationship would become. As Ben and I now progress through our third decade together, I rejoice over the fruitfulness and longevity of our partnership. Ben Dailey has become my son-in-the-Lord and my friend for life.

I'm delighted that Ben has shared the story of his spiritual journey through this book, *Limitless*. His vulnerability is amazing. In this book, he opens the curtains and allows the reader a full, unobstructed look into his heart. He's willing to run the risk of being misunderstood or criticized in order to share the full impact of his life-transforming journey. Ben wants everyone who reads this book to experience a mind-renewing, spirit-revitalizing, life-changing encounter with the God of limitless grace.

The story of Ben's transformation isn't unique. Many others have experienced similar life-renewals by being overwhelmed with the sacrificial, unmerited love of Jesus Christ. Still, the beauty and power of this message is strangely rare. Perhaps some lack the courage and others lack the ability to articulate this beautiful truth. Ben's genuine passion for truth has compelled him to open his heart to others. He hopes their lives will be changed, too, as they are overwhelmed with the grace of God. Ben believes God's provision for each of His children is truly limitless.

Be assured that your *love for* God and your *faith in* God will soar to new heights as you read this book. Get ready to be challenged and changed. An exciting journey in growth and understanding lies before you. That's my promise to you!

My friendship and ministry partnership with Ben continues to strengthen and deepen as the years go by. As you read this book, you'll learn what I've experienced in the years the two of us have been together: Ben Dailey is a man with a bold, daring exterior who possesses a gentle heart of love and compassion. While reading through the pages of this book, you'll see the telltale signs of both his explosive faith and his tender spirit. And, you'll get to know God better than you've ever known Him before.

Be blessed as you take your personal journey into God's amazing grace.

— **J. Don George, founding pastor of Calvary Church, Irving, Texas**

INTRODUCTION

> ❝ That's the big difference between Christianity and other religions. The difference between Works and Grace or Do and Done. ❞
>
> **—Rick Warren**

This is a book I never planned to write. It's a message I didn't even know I needed to hear. I'd been a Christian for decades—by any normal standards, a deeply committed follower of Jesus Christ—but I was seriously misguided. In many ways, I can identify with the blind man who, after Jesus touched him, responded, "I see people; they look like trees walking around." He saw, but he didn't see. It took another touch from Jesus so that "he saw everything clearly" (Mark 8:24–25). When I began to realize what I'd been missing, I could have said, "I once was blind, but now I squint." By the astonishing kindness of God, I see more clearly now. This book is about God's touch in my life—and His touch enabled me to see Jesus.

For many years, I was focused on all I needed to do for God. I worked hard, I did my very best, and I poured out my life to serve Him, but it became a grinding duty without beauty. I can't pinpoint the moment or the season it happened, but the Christian life became more about my performance and my accomplishments *for God* than about His matchless, wondrous love *for me*. When I lost the focus on God's grace, I lost my joy, my strength, my delight, and my security. I became obsessed with proving myself worthy of acclaim, and I compared myself with anyone and everyone. If I was doing better than others by some standard, I felt good—or to be more accurate, I felt proud. If they looked better than me in some area, I was driven at all costs to do better than them—which is a sign of deep insecurity and fear. Legalism is the opposite of grace. It's the belief that we can do enough and be enough to earn God's favor. It focuses on obedience to God's law instead of His forgiveness, love, and power. I'm an expert in legalism—I lived it every day.

For years, my preaching was about seven steps to a better this or that, and my leadership focused on excellence. There's nothing wrong with clear points in a sermon, unless we miss the only point that matters: responding to the amazing grace of Jesus in faith, hope, and love. And there's nothing wrong with excellence, unless it's driven by fear and pride instead of by delight in our great and gracious King. I've learned—and I continue to learn every day—that the Christian life isn't about *what I do* for God, but about *what He's already done* to, in, and for each of us.

People need help with their marriages, but they need Jesus more. They need help managing their money, but they need Jesus even more. They need guidance to raise their kids, but they need Jesus even more. He is the source, the light, our righteousness, our security, our strength, and our great delight. He is our life.

This isn't a new truth. God assured a timid and anxious Abram, later named Abraham, "Do not be afraid, Abram. I am your shield, your very great reward" (Gen. 15:1). We long for security; God has promised to be our shield in adversity. We long for true wealth and meaning; God has given us the greatest treasure imaginable—Himself.

But I had missed the point. I had read and taught the Bible, prayed and served faithfully, but I had missed *Him*. Actually, I had tried to use God as a tool to help me accomplish my goals, but I discovered that God doesn't want to be a tool. He wants to be my tender, loving Father and powerful King.

Doctrine and Experience

Accurate doctrine about God is essential, but it's not enough. We need to grasp what the doctrines are saying about a personal God who has done everything to convince us that He loves us. We need to study the Bible and absorb good teaching, but those truths should lead us to a genuine encounter with the risen, fully alive Savior. Then, the truths of the Bible aren't sterile words on a page; we have a sense of Christ's presence, pardon, and power in our hearts—and nothing is ever the same again.

I know plenty of people who are avid students of the Bible, but many of them are like me. Somehow, knowledge of the Bible got in the way of knowing God. Jesus told the Pharisees, "You study the Scriptures diligently because you think that in them you have eternal life. These are the very Scriptures that testify about me" (John 5:39). Then and now, many people see the Bible as a manual for living but they don't truly know Emmanuel.

Too many of us (and I'm chief among us) have seen ourselves primarily as God's slaves who were obligated to obey Him . . . or else! We gave, we served, and we sang, but primarily out of a sense of duty. When Paul wrote his letter to the Galatians, he corrected their misguided thinking that duty to God was the supreme motivation. He told them bluntly that they had missed it all. He said they were "foolish" to believe such things. Then he assured them of a different—a radically different—way to relate to God: "Because you are his sons, God sent the Spirit of his Son into our hearts, the Spirit who calls out, *'Abba*, Father.' So you are no longer a slave, but God's child; and since you are his child, God has made you also an heir" (Gal. 4:6–7).

As I've taught the concepts in this book, I've seen a wide range of reactions:

- Some people are thrilled to experience more love, freedom, and joy than they ever thought possible.

- Many people are confused, at least initially. All their lives, they've gone to church and been taught that they need to perform to earn God's acceptance. To them, the message of grace seems like a foreign language. They recognize some words and ideas, but the basic thrust of the message is against everything they've understood about God, themselves, and the Christian life. Sooner or later, though, most of these people come to the glorious realization that God's grace is really true!

- A few people have gotten angry with me about my message of God's unconditional love and acceptance. They've based their lives on performing well enough to merit God's approval. They've poured out blood, sweat, tears, and untold hours of effort to prove themselves worthy. "Who are you," they ask in words or scowls, "to tell me that I've been wrong all this time? Look at all I've done for God!"

- And of course, some people who have already been gripped by the grace of God have been delighted that I finally got it. They've said, "Yes, it's true! Isn't Jesus magnificent!" (And they probably wondered, *Ben, what took you so long*?)

The message of God's grace has always been the most stunning, liberating, and motivating truth the world has ever heard, but it's exceedingly hard to grasp. Everything in us resists it. We'd rather prove ourselves than receive a free gift from God. In fact, all the letters of the New Testament are attempts to convince skeptical Christians that the grace of God is abundant and life changing. It transforms our motivation to obey. We're no longer fearful, driven slaves, but beloved children who long to delight our Father.

The goal of this book isn't to make people angry, but it's inevitable that a few will become incensed by the message of grace. Jesus shook up the Pharisees by insisting that following rules isn't enough to experience God, and pagans and Jews beat Paul for teaching this message. I don't expect to be beaten, but I think there will be plenty of raised eyebrows and a few people muttering under their breath. (And a few might post their angry comments on their blogs.)

We were created for a rich, warm, challenging, stimulating relationship with God. Sin caused a cataclysmic disruption, but God didn't give up on us. He went to the greatest lengths imaginable to reach out to us and draw us back to Himself. We can't earn His love; we can only gratefully receive it, bask in it, and let it change us from the inside out.

When the Christian life is about our duty, our performance, and our need to prove ourselves, it becomes a grind. We live by comparison, fear, and pride. Our focus is on us instead of the One who demonstrated His great love by sacrificing Himself for us.

Trusting in our own efforts to win God's favor may take different forms in different people. The categories include proving, pleasing, and hiding.

- Proving—Some of us are determined to do enough. We live by rules, written and unwritten, and we're fiercely committed to follow them, to achieve our goals, and to show that we're worthy.

- Pleasing—Others among us are more relational than goal-oriented in our self-justification. When someone has a need, we do everything possible to meet it. We gravitate to broken, needy people because fixing their problems makes us feel strong and connected. Feeling indispensable gives us a sense of value.

- Hiding—Some of us are so wounded and afraid that we can't imagine taking any risk of trying to accomplish something or please anyone. We feel so insecure that we try to blend into the wallpaper so no one will notice. To be honest, we may have tried really hard in the past to live up to someone's high standards or please a demanding person, but we failed. We felt so crushed that we concluded the only reasonable solution was never trying again.

Proving, pleasing, and hiding. Actually, these aren't completely separate categories of the ways we've tried to cope with the drive to prove ourselves and ease the gnawing pain of not measuring up. Many of us try different strategies in different situations or with different people. For instance, we may be driven at work, fearfully compliant with our spouse, or determined to hide from people who criticize and dominate us. For most of us, it's a mixed bag—a toxic mixed bag. For years, we've assumed the answer was to work harder, please even more, or hide more effectively—but it hasn't worked out very well. There has to be another way.

The grace of God blows up our misunderstanding, our false pride, and our secret fears. When we get a glimpse of His amazing love and the fact that He has already done everything to make us secure, beloved sons and daughters, we laugh with joy and weep with delight. We realize God's grace is limitless, and our experience of Him knows no bounds.

Paul prayed for the Ephesians to have an experience of the love of God that would blow the sides off their boxes. It is my prayer for you as well.

> My response is to get down on my knees before the Father, this magnificent Father who parcels out all heaven and earth. I ask him to strengthen you by his Spirit— not a brute strength but a glorious inner strength—that Christ will live in you as you open the door and invite him in. And I ask him that with both feet planted firmly on love, you'll be able to take in with all followers of Jesus the extravagant dimensions of Christ's love. Reach out and experience the breadth! Test its length! Plumb the depths! Rise to the heights! Live full lives, full in the fullness of God. God can do anything, you know—far more than you could ever imagine or guess or request in your wildest dreams! He does it not by pushing us around but by working within us, his Spirit deeply and gently within us. (Eph. 3:14–20, MSG)

No, these aren't just words on a page, and Paul's desire for the Ephesians wasn't a pipedream. Paul prayed that they would be *blown away* by the love of God precisely because they—and we—tended to settle for something far, far less. The life-changing experience Paul desired for the Ephesians is the same that God wants for you and me. It's *limitless*. Nothing less.

In this book, and even more, in my life, I want people to see Jesus, to hear His voice and sense His kindness. My message has become: Look *to* Him and look *at* Him. Don't substitute doing things for Him for truly knowing Him. On every page of this book, I hope you'll be staggered by the relentless, unwavering grace of God. I hope you'll respond to His love by loving Him in return.

This book is the story of my frustration, my exasperation, my exhaustion . . . and my discovery that Jesus is more than enough to fill my heart with an ocean of His love, forgiveness, and acceptance. The first chapter, though, will give some background to my desperation.

Put bluntly, the American church today accepts grace in theory but denies it in practice. We say we believe that the fundamental structure of reality is grace, not works—but our lives refute our faith.

— **Brennan Manning**

---

1 DRIFT

> God cannot give us a happiness and peace
> apart from himself, because it is not there.
> There is no such thing.
>
> **—C. S. Lewis**

I'm not sure what happened, how it happened, or even when it happened. All I know is that I drifted.

I grew up watching my parents walk with God. My father was a pastor, and I had the greatest respect for him. When my mom and dad experienced fierce and unjustified opposition from church people, I blamed God. For years, I stayed angry with God for letting my parents suffer unjustly. Then, during the summer after I graduated from high school, God met me late at night in a shed behind my parents' house. It had been converted into a bedroom, and He shook up my world! The love of God flooded my heart. I had the sheer joy of sensing God's kindness, His power, and His presence.

At the time, I didn't have theological words to describe my experience, but it didn't matter—the love of Jesus was so real I could touch and taste it! He was alive and real to me, and I was fully alive to Him. It wasn't like I was walking around in a daze. It was just the opposite. I was acutely aware of God's presence and my new purpose in life. I was overwhelmed with the question, "How could God love someone like me so much?" It was a question I loved to consider because it always led me back to the wonder of His grace.

I was aware that this revelation of God's love was a gift from His hand to me. I hadn't earned a thing. I had been angry, rebellious, and sullen, but God reached into this darkness with His tender hand of love. At the deepest part of my heart, God worked the miracle of healing and restoration. My repentance wasn't coerced by guilt or shame. God had invited me to come to Him, to lay down my resentment and bask in the warmth of His kindness. I repented because I sensed His great love for me.

Conflicting Messages

When Jesus met me in the shed behind my parents' house, I was captivated by the love of God. Obeying Him wasn't a dry, empty, forced obligation. I wanted to please the one who loved me so much, and I was glad to do anything He asked me to do! But as I moved away from home and listened to all kinds of messages—in Bible school, to preachers on television, and in church each week—I heard two different messages. One said that God loves us unconditionally, His grace is free, and repentance puts us in touch with the wonder of His affection for us. This is the message that was given to unbelievers to assure them of the truth of the gospel.

The other message was for believers, and it was quite different. In many ways, this message said,

"You'd better obey, or else."

"You aren't committed enough."

"You aren't good enough for God."

"You'd better try harder."

"You need to be more disciplined."

"You'd better follow the examples of the heroes in the
   Bible . . . and don't be like those unfaithful people!"

"You're not praying enough, giving enough, or serving
   enough to really please God."

It doesn't take too many of these messages to convince us
that we're walking a tightrope with God, and we'd better do
everything just right to stay on. One little slip and . . .

Ironically, unbelievers are attracted to the unconditional,
wonderful grace of God, but too many believers live in bondage
and guilt, assuming they can never measure up to God's standards. They've completely missed the ongoing grace God wants
to pour into their hearts and lives. It almost seems better for
people to remain unbelievers and be drawn to God's grace than
to become legalistic, moralistic, guilt-driven churchgoers.

These messages weren't abstract to me. I internalized them
until they became my identity, my reason to live, and my heart's
motivation. Grace vanished. I believed I wasn't good enough for
God, and I'd better try harder—much harder—if I had any hope
of staying on His good side. Somehow, I had to earn His love
and acceptance.

When I first trusted Christ, my obedience was an overflow
of my experience of the love of God. Gradually, however, my
obedience became a measuring stick that determined if I was
a good enough person and, more precisely, a good enough
Christian. I compared myself with others around me to see how I
was stacking up. If I was serving more than they were serving, or
if I had more emotional intensity than they did, I felt good about
myself. I was winning! It was nothing but pride. When I failed,
or when I saw others succeed, I felt the toxic blend of shame,

envy, fear, and resentment. Oh, I never talked about those feelings and perceptions. No one really talked about them, but they
were as real as anything in the world.

Instead of finding the right answer and letting

the love of God transform my heart, I

doubled-down on my efforts to prove worthy

of His acceptance.

Some people might read this and ask, "Well, Ben, why
didn't you go back to the grace of God and experience His love
again? Why didn't you correct the problem with the truth of the
gospel?" That's a great question, but the solution I heard over
and over again was, "Try harder, do more, be more committed,
and prove yourself to God." Instead of finding the right answer
and letting the love of God transform my heart, I doubled-down
on my efforts to prove worthy of His acceptance. It was a never-
ending rat race.

My drift away from the grace of God was gradual, imper-
ceptible, and complete. All the demanding, condemning,
guilt-inducing messages eventually felt completely normal.
When I was growing up in California, my family often went to
the beach. One day, my brothers and I went out into the waves
on a float. I looked back to the beach and saw other parents
and kids building sandcastles, and I relaxed in the ocean. A little
while later, I looked up, but I didn't recognize where I was. I
scanned the beach. I saw a lot of other families, but I couldn't
see my family. I got out and looked around. I had drifted a half
a mile up the beach to another part of the coast! I hadn't been
aware that it happened, but it happened nonetheless. That's

what happened to me when I drifted away from the grace of God and found myself living by the demands of performance. Every church that lives by performance has its own list of requirements. They used to be "don't cuss, don't drink, and don't dance," but today, they are more likely to be "give enough, attend often enough, serve till you're exhausted, pray with passion, fast until you're sick, and be absolutely sure about everything." But I knew my heart, and I knew things about my deepest desires that weren't what God wanted. I put on a show to impress others, and I often succeeded, but I was secretly sure that I could never do enough to impress God. There was just too much junk in my heart. I knew it, and I knew that God knew it.

The problem was that I was a pastor. I was supposed to point people to Jesus, but I had internalized the demanding messages and was communicating them to the staff and people in our church. I had become part of the problem. Leading and pastoring were more about me than about God. I was committed to building a great church, a really big church, a church other pastors would envy. When we didn't grow as fast as I wanted, I became impatient with God's timetable and methods. I started believing I could build Jesus' church better than Jesus could!

I became committed to doing, to proving, to achieving, but I forgot to enjoy the unconditional, fathomless love of God. I lost my joy. I was running on empty—burned out, confused, and furious. Soon, I hated the church, I despised serving God, and I resented anyone who asked me to do anything at any time. I also hated someone else: me. I knew I was a colossal failure. I couldn't live up to God's perfect standards, and I couldn't even live up to my own standards. Guilt, self-pity, and shame compounded my confusion and anger. I was a mess.

I recently heard a speaker describe our drive to prove ourselves as *performancism*. The "ism" means it's a philosophy, a belief, a comprehensive way of looking at ourselves and the world. It's not just a minor problem; it leads to a kind of spiritual death because it equates our value to our performance. It is the product of the mindset that what we do, what we have, and all we achieve signal our worth.

Never Enough

Living by performance is much like any other addiction. If you think this comparison is too drastic, let me explain how the addictive cycle works.

- Frustration creates anxiety that cries out for relief. For an alcoholic, life's challenges, combined with the added heartaches caused by the addiction, produce a lot of uneasiness. For the performance addict, the realization of not being enough is a constant source of anxiety.

- Addicts then fantasize about the chemical or behavior that promises relief. A performance addict imagines "the big win" that will impress people.

- Thoughts lead to specific behaviors to pursue the substance or behavior.

- The person engages in the behavior: drinking, drugs, shopping, sex, gambling . . . or performing to earn approval. The promise is that this activity will ease frustration, calm anxiety, and bring the joy they desperately seek.

- The "high" from the drug or the behavior may last for a few moments or a few days, but sooner or later, the person comes down. The person feels empty, alone, and more anxious than before, triggering a new cycle.

I can see now how all the elements of this cycle were working in my own life. Deep feelings of not being good enough triggered fantasies that I could do something to impress Kim, the people on our staff, the people in our church, and maybe even God. I dreamed big dreams of success—but always to stroke my ego and polish my reputation, not to honor God. And I put my dreams into action. When they succeeded, I felt fantastic . . . euphoric . . . superior . . . and arrogant. But the feelings didn't last long. I had to "keep feeding my habit" of success to make me feel good about myself. When I saw others succeed, I felt jealous. I saw them as competitors. Oh, I was slick enough to not appear that I resented their success, but just below the surface, I seethed. When I failed, I had to blame somebody. I often blamed my staff, Kim, God, or anyone but myself. When I couldn't shift the blame, I had to swallow the hard conclusion that I was defective and deficient. I felt waves of crushing shame, which drove me to conclude, "I never want to feel this way again! I'll make sure I succeed next time!" And another cycle kicked into gear.

No matter what I did, I lived with the nagging feeling that it was never enough.

No matter what I did, I lived with the nagging feeling that it was never enough. I worked like a dog, but I was afraid someone was working harder. I was intense in my zeal, but I was afraid someone else was more zealous. I prayed for long periods, but when I said, "Amen," I had a sickening feeling that I hadn't prayed long enough, sincerely enough, or specifically enough.

I relived conversations and beat myself up for saying some-thing stupid or realizing the other person wasn't moved or impressed by what I'd said. When I was at work, I was haunted by the fact that I wasn't the husband and father I needed to be. When I was at home, my mind was consumed with all the things I needed to do back at the office. When I went to my kids' sports events, I sometimes left at halftime because I couldn't stand feeling unproductive. My mind and heart were always consumed with the next thing I needed to do to be successful. I was so driven to accomplish things that I could never relax and just be "in the moment" with my wife, my kids, my friends, or my God. In fact, when we planted a church when our daughter Kyla was a little girl, I was totally absorbed with getting the church up and running. Today, I don't have any memories of her from the time she was three until she was six. It's not that I had a lobotomy and I'm missing those memories. I don't have any memories of her because I wasn't with her enough for the memories to even exist.

Receiving and Giving

God has called us to give love and joy to others out of the abundance of the grace He has given to us. In one of the feasts in Jerusalem, Jesus watched each day as the ceremonies of washings and sacrifices rose to a crescendo on the last day. John gives us a picture of the drama at the feast:

> On the last and greatest day of the festival, Jesus stood and said in a loud voice, "Let anyone who is thirsty come to me and drink. Whoever believes in me, as Scripture has said, rivers of living water will flow from within them." By this he meant the Spirit. (John 7:37–39)

The Christian life is meant to be a continual filling of God's love, wisdom, and strength by the presence of the Holy Spirit

(Eph. 5:18). As God fills us and we overflow, we give, love, and serve those around us—not to get something from them to fill our emptiness, but out of the abundance of our fullness. The filling we need isn't church attendance or duties or service. We need to drink deeply of Jesus Himself, the living water. Only then can the river of living water flow from deep within us into the lives of others.

During my time of spiritual drought, another passage about water characterized my life. God spoke through the prophet Jeremiah to wake up His people:

"My people have committed two sins:
They have forsaken me,
the spring of living water,
and have dug their own cisterns,
broken cisterns that cannot hold water." (Jer. 2:13)

I had been created (and recreated) by God to be a channel of the living water of Christ, but I had dried up. A cistern has no external source to fill it. It isn't a spring, and it isn't a well. It's just a container that holds the water poured into it. I had drifted away from the "spring of living water" to dig my own cistern. I felt like I was dying of spiritual thirst, but I had the wrong solution. I worked like crazy, ramped up my intensity, and tried to dig a huge cistern to hold water—but it couldn't; it was broken. No matter how hard I tried, I was still cracked and empty. Every time I tried to pour nourishing, refreshing water into my life through prayer and Bible study, it immediately leaked out. My life was all about my efforts to perform instead of finding Jesus refreshing.

The Scriptures use another liquid, oil, as an additional metaphor for spiritual life. Jesus told us, "You are the light of the world" (Matt. 5:14). The source of light is the oil in the lamp, and oil is a symbol of the presence of the Holy Spirit. I had been giving, serving, and laboring so hard and so long that my light was flickering and dim. The oil in my lamp was extremely low because I wasn't replenishing it with the love and grace of God. I couldn't be a light when the oil of intimacy with God was so low.

All a Grind

I knew these passages of Scripture (and many others) about the need to experience God's love before expressing it to others, but the loud, noisy messages of performance drowned out God's whisper inviting me to come back to enjoy Him. When I felt desperate, empty, ashamed, and afraid (yes, all at the same time!), I tried even harder. I read the Bible, but only to get a word I could preach to impress people, not to find the true treasure of Christ. I prayed—but to ask God to bless my ministry so I could be more successful and ease the pain in my heart, not to know Him more intimately and find rest in His arms. I spent long hours planning and pulling off events and services, but there was no joy in it. When I got home, Kim wanted to spend time with me, but I saw her as an annoyance who asked too much of me, and in fact, often got in the way of my success. Kyla and Kade wanted their daddy, but I was too consumed with accomplishing great things for God to be the loving father God wanted me to be. No matter where I went, I was sure I needed to be somewhere else. No matter what I did, it was never enough.

I lived on a treadmill of discouragement about my failures and false hopes that if I just tried harder, I'd make it the next time. I just needed to be more committed. I needed to give more and do more. The next success, I was convinced, would bring true joy and meaning. But no matter how well things went, the successes never filled the hole in my heart. I was never quite good enough—actually, *never even close* to good enough. But I kept trying. Life was a long, excruciating grind.

My drift away from the wonder of grace left me anxious, insecure, and hyper-controlling.

My drift away from the wonder of grace left me anxious, insecure, and hyper-controlling. For me, people and situations almost always felt out of control. The haunting prospect of failure and uncertainty about the future drove me to put my hands on every decision, and in fact, every person's mood all the time. I was always on, noticing everything—because everything was a potential threat! I was sure I just needed to be more diligent, more on top of things, and more insistent. This pathological obsession drove me nuts, and it drove people away from me . . . including those I love most.

Every culture has its own language, and the performance culture has one too. I listened to leaders who try to inspire us but often have a demanding tone and tell us to "give it all for God," to live in "radical obedience," to "give until it hurts," and to "be sold out for Jesus." All of these statements can be understood in the context of grace, but that's not how I heard them. They drove my engines to do more to prove myself . . . always more.

In all my efforts, I saw plenty of successes and a few failures. God was doing amazing things, but I couldn't see His hand. I didn't see His power and love working through me. I thought it was all about me just grinding out life and ministry. I couldn't enjoy the successes because I was haunted by every flaw—large or small, real or perceived. The highs quickly evaporated, and the lows devastated me. I began critiquing everybody and everything, but not with a dispassionate eye. I felt condemned, so I condemned everything and everybody. Even when we saw God do amazing things—lives changed, people saved, the hungry fed, and God at work in other wonderful ways—I focused on what went wrong. My sour demeanor poisoned my relationship with Kim. She dreaded seeing me after every service and event because I inevitably ripped them to shreds. Week after week, I watched her countenance drop at lunch as I tore into what went wrong and who failed. In the services, she had been thrilled to see God do amazing things, but my criticisms turned her joy into discouragement.

For some people, the pervasive fear of failure and rejection soon leads to depression; for others, it produces an even more intense push to succeed—and no one had better get in the way! People walked on eggshells around me. At home, Kim knew the subjects that were off-limits, and she coached the kids to avoid talking to me about those things—and to avoid me completely at certain times of the week. Before the weekend services, Kim reminded them to leave me alone because I was preparing. After the services, no matter how well they went, I was harsh and critical. The look on my face screamed to my children, "Stay away!" My staff were always on edge, wondering if a single wrong word might set me off. However, outside my close circle of family and staff, most people saw me as completely calm, happy, and in control. At least, that's the image I tried desperately to portray to them.

I became so raw and wounded that I overreacted to any perceived slight, and I resented any demand on my time. Every command from God became offensive, and I was deaf to any invitation to come close and enjoy His love.

I'd like to think this wrong perception of life and God was unique to me, but it's not. As I've talked about my misguided assumptions, many others have said, "Ben, that's me too!" Christians in every walk of life—people in business, doctors, nurses, engineers, accountants, farmers, teachers, housewives, and all the rest—can lose their focus on Christ, and when they lose Him, they lose heart. The irony is that the more driven we are to prove ourselves as "good Christians," the farther we move from the source of love, joy, and light. In *The Sacred Romance*, Brent Curtis and John Eldredge comment:

> To lose heart is to lose everything. And a "loss of heart" best describes most men and women in our day. It isn't just the addictions and affairs and depression and heartaches, though God knows, there are enough of these to cause even the best of us to lose heart. But there is the busyness, the drivenness, the fact that most of us are living merely to survive. Beneath it we feel restless, weary and vulnerable.[1]

What If?

During my darkest season of feeling restless, weary, and vulnerable, I kept looking for the key that would fix everything. I wrote messages on "Three Keys to Success," "How to Lead When You're on Empty," and "Twenty-One Days to Victory." I went to seminars on how to be a better father, husband, pastor, and friend. I hoped someone somewhere could give me the answer. I searched everywhere to find the principle, the book, the conference, the concept, the *anything* that would fill the emptiness. They all made glowing promises, so I tried them all. But nothing worked. I was dying inside. It was like a carrot on a stick. Every time I seemed to get close to true fulfillment, the joy of love and life remained just out of reach. Legalism is exhausting because it promises so much but delivers so little. You feel like you're getting close, but it's an empty promise. It's a carrot we can never quite put our hands on.

Actually, my attempts to implement all the principles only made me feel more discouraged than ever. The speakers and writers told how their lives had been transformed by the points they shared, but their concepts did nothing for me. I concluded that I was utterly, completely hopeless. At these events, I spent time with some of the speakers, and I discovered many of them were just as burned out as I was. Actually, these conversations made me feel a little better . . . after all, misery loves company.

Gradually, I realized there was no quick fix to my problems. I was in a desert, but I had no idea I was in the exact place where I could find a spring of water. I began to ask hard questions . . . good questions . . . questions that would eventually lead to an awakening in my life. I wondered,

- What if the cross of Jesus Christ is enough?

- Is it possible to experience true joy?

- How does the Holy Spirit provide assurance, comfort, and strength?

- Jesus' last words on the cross were, "It is finished" (John 19:30). What if it's really true? What if Jesus really meant what He said? Can I simply rest in His finished work?

- What if there is something different about the Old and New Covenants?

- How can I understand the connection between law and grace?

These questions were like a splash of cold water in my face. I had drifted, but it was time for the drifting to stop. I needed to listen to the writer of Hebrews who encourages us, "We must pay the most careful attention, therefore, to what we have heard, so that we do not drift away" (Heb. 2:1).

I had tried everything to prove myself worthy of God's love, and I had tried desperately to impress people to win their applause. When I failed over and over again, I tried even harder. Now, it was time to try something else. But I had to come to the ultimate, absolute end before I could begin.

God's grace is painted on the canvas of despair.

—T. D. Jakes

Consider this . . .

1. Look at John 7:37–39. What does it look like and feel like when a person "drinks the living water" of Jesus so deeply that he or she overflows with love, compassion, wisdom, joy, and strength?

2. On a scale of 0 (not at all) to 10 (all day every day), how much does Jesus' description of the overflowing life in John 7 characterize your experience right now? Explain your answer.

3. Why do you think it seems so normal to try to live the Christian life by proving ourselves to God and impressing others? What are the results when it looks like we're succeeding? And when we're failing?

4. What are some examples of how people try to prove themselves, please to win approval, and hide from any risk and conflict? Which of these have you tried? What were the results?

5. Paraphrase this statement: The irony is that the more driven we are to prove ourselves as "good Christians," the farther we move from the source of love, joy, and light.

6. What is God saying to you in this chapter?

2 THE END AND THE BEGINNING

> We Christians cannot talk about loving God until we come to grips with our raging passion for ourselves. We cannot and will not love anyone but ourselves until we meet God in a way that stirs us to race after him with single-minded intensity, until our deepest desire is to get to know him better. I must surrender my fascination with myself to a more worthy preoccupation with the character and purposes of God. I am not the point. He is.

—Dr. Larry Crabb

One Sunday after church, I took my family and our staff out to lunch. Somewhere in the middle of sandwiches and chips, we began to talk about the crushing burden of living by performance. We began to recount the language of oppressive motivations, the "have tos" and the "you'd betters." Someone mentioned the passage where Jesus told His followers, "Whoever wants to be my disciple must deny themselves and take up their cross and follow me" (Matt. 16:24).

I snapped, "Doesn't God see that I'm doing enough? I'm already carrying this ministry, the expectations of our people and the community, the financial concerns of our church, and the needs of my family—and I'm failing at all of them! How in the world can I carry anything else! I can't. I just can't do it!"

I was not alone. In fact, I had made sure I was not alone in carrying the burdens! I had demanded more of our staff than anyone had a right to ask, and I had been very stingy in my compliments. I felt driven and condemned, and I had spread that poison to everyone on our team. That day at lunch, I saw it in their eyes.

A quick lunch turned into a phenomenal four-hour meeting of hearts and minds. As we were honest with each other, virtually all of us cried deep tears. We felt understood, we felt loved, and for the first time in a long, long time, we had a glimmer of hope that life could be different.

Each in our own way, we articulated a common question: What if the good news is really good news? This question led to many others. How could the magnificent message of God's love and forgiveness that draws people to faith become so distorted that it produces fear, guilt, and shame in the lives of sincere Christians? That makes no sense, but it was the shared experience of almost everyone at the table . . . everyone but Kim. She hadn't grown up in the church, so she hadn't been inundated with all the "shoulds," "oughts," and "have tos." She knew the grace of God had rescued her from sin and death, and she was thrilled to follow the One who loved her so much. For the rest of us, the good news was about past forgiveness and present demands, but for Kim, it was grace first, last, and always.

As I looked at the Scriptures, I realized what was happening at our table was a carbon copy of the people who encountered Jesus. Some of the people described in the Gospels were like

Kim, new to the faith with little or no religious background, but others were outcasts and misfits. All of these people gladly embraced Jesus and His message of grace. The religious people, the ones who had been steeped in messages about God and tradition, almost universally resisted Jesus' love. In the Gospels, this group (and the ones like them at our table) were so tied to rules, self-justification, and self-validation that they couldn't accept God's wonderful, free gift that was standing right in front of them!

The gospels paint this contrast on page after page. We could look at many passages, but one represents the rest. The parable of the prodigal son is probably the most famous story Jesus told, but we might overlook Luke's description of the actual scene when Jesus told this story. He wrote, "Now the tax collectors and sinners were all gathering around to hear Jesus. But the Pharisees and the teachers of the law muttered, 'This man welcomes sinners and eats with them'" (Luke 15:1–2).

There was something about Jesus that attracted the people no one in polite society wanted around. Tax collectors weren't like our IRS agents today who have respectable jobs working for the government. In first-century Palestine, these were Jewish people who collaborated with the Roman forces to extort exorbitant taxes from their own people to fund the occupiers. They were considered traitors. They were the most despised people in the country, but they felt welcomed by Jesus. The sinners weren't garden-variety liars and gossips; they were prostitutes and pimps. Today, they'd also include drug dealers, thieves, and the criminal underground. They, too, sensed that Jesus loved them in spite of their flaws.

The religious elite had elaborate rituals to prevent any contact with "those people," and they detested Jesus for spending time with them. But Jesus went further than arm's-length contact—He ate meals with them. In their culture, eating with someone implied complete social acceptance. That's why the religious elite "muttered" with contempt.

The Pharisees tried to control Jesus and limit His influence. They argued with Him publicly, and they tried to persuade others to side with them against Him. We often consider them the "bad guys" in the story, but actually, they were upholding the truth of the Bible and devotion to God in a world that was crumbling under the oppression of Roman occupation. Their goal was noble, but their method was tragically wrong. They insisted on rules, demands, and condemnation as the means to control people's behavior—including their own.

As our staff team talked that long afternoon at the restaurant, I realized I had become a card-carrying Pharisee. I was devoted to the Bible and religious tradition, but I had missed Jesus. Was the good news good for all of life, not just a doorway to heaven? Could the gospel of grace apply to me all day every day so that it freed me from my addiction to performance and lifted the cloud of fear and shame? Could the promises of peace and rest be real for me? Could I get off the treadmill of performance and hyper-control and enjoy God and the freedom He offers? Could I stop digging my cistern and turn to drink deeply of the living water of Jesus?

I realized there was another set of questions that challenged me to the core: *If I'm not trusting in all my accomplishments to impress God and people, what happens to my identity? Who will I be?* I had lived to make people sit up and take notice, but if my heart became filled and overflowing with delight in the love of Jesus, I knew everything would change—everything that's important, anyway.

God had to show me the incredible depths of
my pursuit of wrong things so I could replace
them with His grace and truth.

A Look in the Mirror

For God to reconstruct my life, He had to blast before He
could build. God had to show me the incredible depths of my
pursuit of wrong things so I could replace them with His grace
and truth. In this season of vulnerability, God used Paul's letters
to shine His light on my misguided desire to measure up. I especially devoured Galatians, Colossians, and Romans. It was as
though I had never read them before. Suddenly, I saw the truth
of God's wonderful grace. He enabled me to look in the mirror
and see more clearly than ever that my identity was tied to the
wrong horse.

A familiar passage took on new meaning. A religious leader,
an expert in the law, asked Jesus, "Teacher, which is the greatest
commandment in the Law?"

He replied, "'Love the Lord your God with all your heart and
with all your soul and with all your mind.' This is the first and
greatest commandment. And the second is like it: 'Love your
neighbor as yourself.' All the Law and the Prophets hang on
these two commandments" (Matt. 22:36–40).

The expert asked Jesus about a law, but Jesus pointed to
love. Where does this kind of love come from? Not from me.
For years, I tried my best to love God with all my heart, and
I failed miserably. I tried to love others to prove I was a good
Christian, and I failed every time. I was drawing on the wrong
source. In his first letter, John explained, "In this is love, not that
we loved God, but that He loved us and sent His Son to be the

propitiation for our sins. Beloved, if God so loved us, we also ought to love one another" (1 John 4:10–11 NASB).

None of us can love—either God or people—by trying harder. Our abject and repeated failure can lead us to one of two conclusions: try even harder and cover up the shame of failure, or turn to an overflowing well of love found in the atoning sacrifice of Jesus Christ that completely satisfies our debt of sin. The cross tells us that we're weak, helpless, and hopeless apart from God's magnificent grace. The cross also tells us that real life doesn't come from us reaching, always stretching to do more to prove ourselves to God, but that Jesus stretched out His hands to bear all the punishment our sins deserve. When we begin to grasp the reality that "we can't do enough" but "God already has done it for us," we'll be overwhelmed with His love.

When God floods us with His kindness, His acceptance, and His glory, then and only then will we love Him in return. Out of the abundance of our experience of His love for us, we love others. To the expert in the law, Jesus articulated the two most important commandments in the Bible, and they're both about love.

During this season of revelation about God's grace, I read Paul's letters, and I came to a startling but undeniable conclusion: I loved something else—prestige, power, and position. As the Holy Spirit caused the scales to fall from my spiritual eyes, I realized my goal in life hadn't been to love God and people at all; it was *image management*. I wanted to look good to the people I thought were important—and that included almost everybody!

For years, I'd talked to friends, read books, listened to messages, and attended conferences to get information about how to be more successful. Why? So that people would be more impressed with me. I wanted to network with other leaders and get to know them. Why? Because I desperately wanted to be seen as an insider. In every interaction with old friends and as I met each person, I secretly sized them up: *I'm a little better than this guy, but that one is more respected than me. I'd better say something really impressive!*

Without a firm grounding in the gospel of grace, I didn't love God with all my heart, and I saw people as competition or stepping-stones to further success. I was insecure and driven. I analyzed every conversation and measured myself by every seminar, workshop, and person I met.

For years, I didn't realize that in every conversation, I mentally scanned every person I met and put them on a measuring stick. I felt superior to some and inferior to others. My heart was clouded by arrogance and fear. It wasn't consumed with love for God and for the people I met. I wanted to make some close friends, but you can't be a friend if you see people as threats to avoid or tools to make you more successful.

When I compared my real goals, desires, and perceptions with the Great Commandment, I realized I was way off-base. I had missed it all. I had been playing a game, competing to win, but even when I felt superior, I still lost. It was all about me.

I realized I had based my security, my identity, and my value on my ability to impress people and God.

Not the Only One

My look in the mirror shattered my world. I realized I had based my security, my identity, and my value on my ability to impress people and God. I had lived by rules—God's rules of righteousness and my rules of success—and I had failed miserably.

In Jesus' story of the prodigal, we often focus on the father's gracious welcome of the wayward younger brother who "came to his senses" and returned home. The father didn't blast him for being such a selfish fool, and he didn't even remind the young man of his sins. In fact, the father interrupted his son's carefully rehearsed confession to welcome him warmly and reinstate him into the family. But there was another brother, the one who stayed and worked on the family farm while his brother wasted his inheritance. When his younger brother returned, this man was in the fields working hard. When he heard the celebration begin, he asked what was going on. A servant explained that his brother had returned and his father was throwing a feast! The older brother was furious and refused to join the party.

The father didn't want his older son to miss out on the greatest day in the life of their family. He left the feast and went out into the fields to find his son to invite him to come to the celebration. The older brother barked at his dad,

> "Look! All these years I've been slaving for you and never disobeyed your orders. Yet you never gave me even a young goat so I could celebrate with my friends. But when this son of yours who has squandered your property with prostitutes comes home, you kill the fattened calf for him!" (Luke 15:29–30)

Listen carefully to the older son's message to his dad:

- "Look!" His first word was more than discourteous; it was offensive! He spoke to his father in anger that the elderly man had been so kind to his sinning but repentant son.

- "All these years I've been slaving for you." His whole life, the older son had been the one destined to inherit most of the family fortune. He lived with a loving, devoted, wise father and enjoyed significant wealth. He worked his own land, but he got no joy out of it. Instead, he saw himself as a slave! He was partner in his dad's family business, but to him, it was pure drudgery.

- I've "never disobeyed your orders." To the older brother, every act of service and obedience was a chip he intended to play at some later time. He wasn't serving out of love for his father but to gain leverage over him.

- "You never gave me even a young goat so I could celebrate with my friends." The older brother had always felt cheated, and now that the fatted calf was being served at a feast for a no-good brother who came home, he was furious! This older son had everything, but he enjoyed nothing.

- "This son of yours . . ." The older brother felt superior to his sinful brother. In fact, he despised him so much that he wouldn't even say his name or claim him as his own brother.

Anger, resentment, superiority or inferiority, a victim-mentality . . . these are the inevitable results of a person trying to earn their place instead of enjoying the Father's limitless love and acceptance. For the older son, life was all duty but no beauty. He did all that was required—but he missed his father's love all day every day. The older brother lived in proximity to the treasure of his dad's affection, wisdom, and kindness, but he remained spiritually, emotionally, and relationally destitute. Ironically, the wayward son had been a slave to sin, but was made a beloved son, while the son who had remained at home thought of himself as a slave.

In *The Prodigal God*, Tim Keller summarizes the end of the parable and explains that Christians who act like "elder broth-ers have an undercurrent of anger toward life circumstances, hold grudges long and bitterly, look down on people of other races, religions, and lifestyles, experience life as a joyless, crushing drudgery, have little intimacy and joy in their prayer lives, and have a deep insecurity that makes them overly sensitive to criticism and rejection yet fierce and merciless in condemning others. What a terrible picture!"[2]

Jesus' story ends with the father responding to his older son's hardened heart: "'My son,' the father said, 'you are always with me, and everything I have is yours. But we had to celebrate and be glad, because this brother of yours was dead and is alive again; he was lost and is found'" (Luke 15:31–32). Do you hear the wonderful tenderness in the father's words to his resentful, self-righteous son? He doesn't say, "You ingrate! How can you be so selfish?" Instead, he says, "My son," *teknon* in Greek, which means "my child." He reminded his son that everything left was now his inheritance. The young man considered himself a slave while he was fabulously wealthy! The dad also reminded his son that love, redemption, and restoration are more important than wealth. "We had to celebrate," he told his defiant son, because grace had won over rebellion in his younger son's life.

Jesus ends the story freeze-framed with the dad and son standing in the field. This produces tremendous tension for the people listening to Jesus. Remember, there were two sets of people listening. The pimps, prostitutes, and traitors were delighted to hear that the son from the pigsty was welcomed home, but the true point of the story was for the others who were listening. Jesus was inviting the self-righteous, arrogant, defiant Pharisees to soften their hearts and come to the feast of grace. Some people have wondered what happened after the end of the story. Actually, we know what happened. A few weeks later, these same Pharisees falsely arrested, accused, tried, and convicted Jesus. He had invited them into the celebration of salvation, but they killed Him.

Look again at the father's heart in Jesus' story. Even when the older son was defiant, belligerent, and immobile, the father gently invited him to come to the celebration. This gives me great comfort! God doesn't hate me for being like the older brother. He reaches out His hand and tenderly asks me to experience His kindness, His warmth, and His affection.

As I've talked to people about my journey to reconnect with the Father's love, many have told me, "Me, too, Ben. I see the same low levels of anger, comparison, and resentment that God isn't giving me what I think I deserve. I've served faithfully in the church, and I've tried to help people in my family. I thought all that got me points with God, but He isn't giving me what I want out of life. I've been a slave, and I hate it. I want to be a beloved child."

Virtually all the messages in our lives reinforce our temptation to measure our lives by our performance.

We have to ask: Why do so many Christians live like elder brothers? The answer is that following rules looks easy and attractive, but grace requires humility. Most of us pick the rules! The natural tendency of the human heart is to prove that we're worthy. All the measuring sticks in our culture reinforce this tendency. Advertisements in all our media promise beauty, success, and popularity if we buy the products and use the services. Success at work is measured by performance standards. Friends are made and kept based on unspoken but very real markers: Does my friend make me feel good and look good to those who are watching us? Virtually all the messages in our lives reinforce our temptation to measure our lives by our performance. Too often, the messages we hear at church speak the same pressuring, condemning message—or maybe, even if the message of grace is crystal clear, we don't have ears to hear it.

Some people, like Kim and the inner circle of people who gathered around Jesus to hear Him tell the story of the prodigal, quickly realize that God's grace is the source of security, hope, and forgiveness. Like many other people I've met, I'm like the older brother in Jesus' story—we cling to self-justification as long as we possibly can. We'd rather relentlessly push ourselves, be driven by fear and guilt, and always try harder instead of resting in the matchless love of God. It's dumb, really dumb.

A New Measuring Stick

The people in first-century Corinth were a lot like us. They had all kinds of problems on both ends of the spectrum, from spiritual pride to sexual promiscuity. In the early chapters of Paul's first letter, he appealed to them to live by grace and avoid divisions, factions, and cliques. Some of the people in the church thought they were superior to others because of their connections with celebrities. Imagine that! Others thought they were much smarter than others because they had studied the Greek philosophers. Their measuring sticks were who they knew, what they had accomplished, and their intelligence. As always, their standards of performance caused jealousy and resentment.

Into this quagmire of misguided presumptions, Paul gave them a different way to think about their self-worth. They didn't need a minor course change; they needed radical restructuring . . . just like many of us. Paul explained,

> I care very little if I am judged by you or by any human court; indeed, I do not even judge myself. My

conscience is clear, but that does not make me innocent. It is the Lord who judges me. Therefore judge
nothing before the appointed time; wait until the
Lord comes. He will bring to light what is hidden in
darkness and will expose the motives of the heart.
At that time each will receive their praise from God.
(1 Cor. 4:3–5)

Comparison, image management, and the desire to impress
put us in the courtroom of human opinion—and we are the
accused! Every activity and every interaction are scrutinized, and
at every moment, we have to prove ourselves to the jury, the
people who are watching us and passing judgment.

The people of Corinth considered themselves members of
the jury judging Paul. But Paul told them, "I don't have to be in
the courtroom any longer. I don't care if I'm judged by you or by
anyone else. Your opinion of me doesn't matter. But that's not
all. *My* opinion of me doesn't matter either! The only opinion
that matters is the Lord's."

Paul completely rejected the world's system of evaluation
and measurement of value based on performance. However, we
might wonder, *Is that good news or bad news? After all, what
is the Lord's opinion of me?*

The Bible gives us another courtroom scene. In one way, it's
similar: we're the defendants. But in a very important way, it's
completely different: we have an attorney . . . in fact, the best
two attorneys we could possibly have! In John's first letter, he
addresses the problem of guilt in the lives of Christians. Even
when we're redeemed, we still sin. Some of us are fairly dense,
so conviction of sin doesn't make much of a dent, but others
have very sensitive consciences, and guilt overwhelms us. John
is speaking to the second group. He writes, "My dear children,
I write this to you so that you will not sin. But if anybody does

sin, we have an advocate with the Father—Jesus Christ, the Righteous One. He is the atoning sacrifice for our sins, and not only for ours but also for the sins of the whole world" (1 John 2:1–2). When we sin as Christians, we stand in the Father's courtroom, and the Enemy of our souls accuses us. If we try to offer our performance as our defense, we fail. But we're not alone. Jesus is our advocate, our attorney. When the charge is read, He doesn't tell the Father, "Oh, she didn't mean it. Let her off this time." No, He says, "Your Honor, my client was guilty, but the sentence has already been completely paid. It is finished. In fact, my client has been completely removed from the scene of the crime." God, the judge isn't harsh, He isn't angry, and He doesn't condemn us. He was the one who sent Jesus to die for us, so He delights to remind us that the debt is paid and we're forgiven.

The Father looks at us and smiles, "Debt paid. Case closed. Your sins and your lawless deeds I will remember no longer (Heb. 10:17)."

John reminds his readers, including us, that the basis of our forgiveness isn't our talents or accomplishments, but the "atoning sacrifice" of Christ. On the cross, all the sins committed by every person who ever lived or will live were put on Him. He endured hell for each of us. He paid the price we should have paid but couldn't pay. He died the death we deserved to die. He took it all on Himself. From the moment we trust in Him and receive His forgiveness and new life, we stand confidently in the courtroom because Jesus has paid the full price for us.

But Jesus isn't alone in defending us. Before His arrest, Jesus promised, "I will ask the Father, and he will give you another advocate to help you and be with you forever" (John 14:16). In the courtroom of heaven, Jesus pleads our case as our advocate who sacrificed Himself to pay for our sins. In our hearts, we need to sense the reality of this wonder of grace. The Holy

Spirit is our advocate, our attorney, too. He lives in us, and one of His roles is to make the love, forgiveness, and acceptance of God real in our hearts. In the depths of our souls, the Holy Spirit advocates for the truth of grace.

For me, *the end* was finally giving up on using my performance as a basis of my security, my identity, and my reputation. I tried everything to make it work, but God didn't let performance and pride fill the emptiness in my heart. I finally woke up and realized I'd been wrong . . . so wrong. *The beginning*, a new beginning, started when I looked back at the cross of Jesus Christ. The grace of God had been there all along, but I had been blind. When I saw it again, my heart melted in wonder that God could love me so much, be so patient, and like the father in Jesus' story, tenderly reach out to me and whisper, "My child, come to me. You've tried so hard to impress people, and look where it got you. There's another way. I'm here, and I love you. Walk with Me. Feel the warmth of My love, and let Me convince you that you are My delight."

Remember

Some people have asked, "Ben, what happened to you? How could you have missed it so badly?" There's a simple answer: I forgot. I forgot the wonder of God's grace poured out for me and in me. When people ask questions like this, I'm not defensive. I've got company. When Peter wrote in the first century, a lot of other people needed to be reminded. He explained,

[God's] divine power has given us everything we need for a godly life through our knowledge of him who called us by his own glory and goodness. Through these he has given us his very great and precious promises, so that through them you may participate in the divine nature, having escaped the corruption in the world caused by evil desires. (2 Peter 1:3–4)

That's really good news! When we grasp the grace of God—or rather, when it grasps us—we are plunged into the love and power of God. Our lives begin to change. Peter draws out a process of spiritual growth from goodness (not being an ornery idiot like some of us have been) to the pinnacle of loving even our enemies. Then he explained why this powerful process is often short-circuited:

If you possess these qualities in increasing measure, they will keep you from being ineffective and unproductive in your knowledge of our Lord Jesus Christ. But whoever does not have them is nearsighted and blind, forgetting that they have been cleansed from their past sins. (2 Peter 1:8–9)

Why don't we have immeasurable joy? Because we've forgotten the grace of God. Why are we resentful and complacent instead of thrilled to serve God? Because the sacrifice of Jesus is no longer melting our hearts. Why do we hold grudges and find fault with people for even the smallest offenses? Because the forgiveness God has poured out on us has bounced off hardened hearts. Why is prayer an afterthought and service drudgery? Because we're not amazed that Jesus came to serve us first.

When I forgot, God didn't give up on me. He brought me to the end of myself so I would finally look to Him. All my frustration and discouragement eventually led me to thirst for the one true source of love and acceptance. He was waiting for me all along.

Now, I'm impressed with Jesus' love for me, so I'm not driven to impress people. He has filled up the hole in my soul, so I don't look to my performance or others' opinions to fill it. I can go to conferences, talk to people, and really listen to their stories. When they share victories, I'm genuinely thrilled instead of secretly jealous. When they tell me how they've suffered, I don't feel superior, because I've been there too.

Make no mistake: comparison is a poison.

I've finally been able to see the power and the poison in comparison. It powerfully rivets our attention on our talents, our appearance, and our image, and other people become pawns in our game to look better than the person standing next to us. Make no mistake: comparison is a poison. It ruins our relationships and makes people into objects of ridicule, sources of jealousy, or celebrities on pedestals. Thoughts of self-appraisal consume us and propel us on the rollercoaster ride of superiority and inferiority, arrogance and shame. Grace takes us off this ride.

What About God's Commands?

Some people have been reading this chapter, and their brows are furrowed. I know. I've seen it happen. They want to ask, "But . . . are you saying God's rules, His laws, His holy commandments in both the Old and New Testaments, aren't important?" Some people who have become enamored with God's grace have claimed that God's laws no longer matter. Theologians call this the *antinomian* position. This is a Greek term that means "lawless." These people teach that grace frees

Christians from any obligation to obey the commands regarding morality and ethics.

No, I'm not saying that at all. The antinomian teaching is the polar opposite of legalism, the idea that, in order to really be saved, we must adhere to a strict moral code and so prove ourselves worthy of God's love. Both are wrong. There's another way—not a balance of these two errors, but a third way: a right understanding of law and grace.

God's commands are crucial, but they aren't the final answer. God's laws communicate several important things to us: They tell us about the holiness of God, they show us that we're sinners who fall short and need a Savior, and for believers, they give us instructions about how to please the One who has made us His dear children. Obeying the law doesn't save anyone. And besides, we can't fulfill them all. James wrote, "Whoever keeps the whole law and yet stumbles at just one point is guilty of breaking all of it" (James 2:10). Some of the laws in the Bible are easy to keep. I hardly ever boil a young goat in its mother's milk (Deut. 14:21). But if we have even a shred of self-awareness, we realize we don't love God with all our hearts, souls, and minds, and none of us love our neighbor as ourselves.

Do you disagree with my assessment? Think of the Golden Rule: "So in everything, do to others what you would have them do to you, for this sums up the Law and the Prophets" (Matt. 7:12). And now, go out and care for others with the same devotion, the same creativity, and the same tenacity with which you meet your own needs. You won't make it an hour before you realize you've failed (or you've set your standards of love far below Jesus' sacrificial service for others).

To those who are committed to self-justification, the law is incredibly attractive because it seems to promise that we can count on our talents, intelligence, efforts, and moral goodness to earn points with God. The law is very clear, black and white, do this and don't do that. Its clarity makes us feel safe and in control. It makes us scorekeepers, and we're sure we're going to win! The law feeds our pride, but in the end, it leaves us empty, angry, and confused. Trying to follow the law produces one of two conditions in us: defeat if we're honest and hypocrisy if we're not. There are no other options.

We need to clear up a common misunderstanding. God's laws weren't given to save anyone, even in the Old Testament. Law and love always went together. God gave Moses the Ten Commandments to show people His righteousness and to reveal how far short they fell from fulfilling them, and He gave them the tabernacle, the sacrifices, and His presence in fire and smoke to remind them of His great love and forgiveness. When they heard the conditional statements of the covenant in the Old Testament ("If you fully obey, I'll bless you."), their conclusion was, "I can't possibly do that!" They realized they needed forgiveness and grace. God instituted the sacrificial system as a symbol of the ultimate sacrifice to come. The prophets foretold of a Messiah who would come to save people from sin, evil, and oppression. For centuries, they looked forward to the Messiah's coming! Still, the full measure of the grace of God remained a mystery . . . until the Messiah actually showed up. Jesus fulfilled the conditions of the covenant, and He paid the price for our disobedience. He fully obeyed God, and He gave Himself as the sacrifice for sin. The Old Testament pointed to Jesus all along, but the full measure of truth and grace wasn't understood until Jesus came.

We can follow God's laws for two very different—in fact, *diametrically opposite* reasons: (1) to earn points with God and prove we're worthy, or (2) out of deep gratitude that He loves us and He made us His own even though we're unworthy. Paul captured this new, radical, grace-drenched motivation in many of his letters. One especially beautiful example is in his letter to the Ephesians: "Follow God's example, therefore, as dearly loved children and walk in the way of love, just as Christ loved us and gave himself up for us as a fragrant offering and sacrifice to God" (Eph. 5:1–2). Why do we follow God's example (which Paul outlined in the previous chapter of Ephesians) of speaking the truth, expressing emotions appropriately, giving generously, encouraging people, and forgiving those who have hurt us? Because we have received the full measure of God's wonderful love in the sacrifice of Jesus, even to the point that He has adopted us as His own "dearly loved children," and we want to please Him in every possible way.

Half measures to correct the problem of self-justification won't do. Paul described our relationship to self-effort to prove ourselves to God as a bad marriage to the law (Rom. 7:1–6). We can't be free unless someone dies. But God's law will never die. Jesus said, "For truly I tell you, until heaven and earth disappear, not the smallest letter, not the least stroke of a pen, will by any means disappear from the Law until everything is accomplished" (Matt. 5:18). No, God's law won't die, but there's another solution: we die. Paul explained, "Or don't you know that all of us who were baptized into Christ Jesus were baptized into his death? . . . For we know that our old self was crucified with him so that the body ruled by sin might be done away with, that we should no longer be slaves to sin—because anyone who has died has been set free from sin" (Rom. 6:3, 6–7).

It's easy to forget grace and go back to legalism, self-justification, and image management. I'm encouraged that the writers of the New Testament kept coming back to God's amazing grace over and over, as the basis of salvation, the glory of a transformed heart, the wonder of a new status as God's beloved children, and the source of a new motivation to live for God—out of gladness instead of guilt. The people in the first century obviously needed to be reminded over and over again, and so do I.

The Shock of Grace

God's grace seems too good to be true. In fact, if the thought of God's unconditional love and acceptance for those who don't deserve it doesn't amaze us, we haven't grasped it yet. Grace is always stunning. The default of the human heart is to try to find something to do to show that we're worthy. God says, "Go ahead and try. Nothing you do can take away your sin or impress Me. You can't feel sorry enough, beat yourself up enough, or say enough prayers to earn forgiveness. And you can't give and serve enough to earn any points with Me. When you give up on all your trying, reach out and take My gift of love, forgiveness, and kindness. It's all about the gift, not about you trying so hard."

Grace transforms those who experience it, but it infuriates those who insist on proving themselves.

Grace transforms those who experience it, but it infuriates those who insist on proving themselves. When Jesus lived, loved, taught and performed miracles, He never elicited a bland response. Today, secular people often say Jesus was "a great teacher" or "a gifted leader," and they list Him along with a dozen other religious leaders. In His day, however, people either adored Him, feared Him, or hated Him. No one just thought He was a "nice" person they could take or leave.

Those who come close to grace have the same dramatic responses. As I've spoken to churches and individuals, many have wept because they are finally convinced that the God of glory delights in them. They don't have to live in fear and guilt any longer. Jesus has paid it all! But others have responded like the Pharisees. They are offended that I (or anyone else) might suggest that all their giving and serving hasn't given them any leverage with God. To be sure, it's gotten them plenty of leverage in their churches. The people watching them may be impressed, but when I tell them God isn't impressed with all their efforts, they get angry. They're sure I'm wrong, and they find others who agree with them.

Grace humbles us because we have to admit that we're empty and our efforts to twist God's arm are worthless. We stop grasping with our hands and simply hold them out to accept the gift of unconditional love. But grace also gives us the highest validation because the God of glory, the Creator of the universe, values us so much that He sent His Son to ransom us back from slavery and adopt us into His family.

Fear and pride keep grace away; humility and gratitude open the door to the wonder of God's tender mercies.

For a variety of reasons, some people believe that God's grace reaches and changes other people, but not them. They have no trouble trusting that others can experience God's grace, but it seems foreign to them. They read the passages and sing the songs, but "the sense of Christ on the heart" still feels distant and unreachable. I was one of those people. When I preached about grace and the experience of God's love, I was sure others would experience it as they trusted in Him, but my heart remained locked in a prison of doubt, pride, and shame. It took a lot for God to break down those prison walls and reach into my heart, but thank God, He did.

When we use the word *gospel*, many Christians relegate the concept to "back then when I trusted Christ." They don't think it applies to anyone after the moment of conversion. That's a tragic misunderstanding. One writer commented that the gospel of grace isn't the diving board to get into the pool; the gospel is the pool we swim in all day every day. The unmerited favor of God, the promise of forgiveness, and the power of the Spirit aren't just the experience to get us into the pool. We need to bathe in the kindness, supernatural power, sovereign purposes, and steadfast hope of the gospel all day every day. To change the metaphor, the gospel of grace isn't just step one of the Christian life; it's the heart and soul of every step in the journey.

We need to correct another misunderstanding: The gospel isn't just a second or third or fourth chance for me to try harder to earn God's grudging acceptance. It doesn't just temporarily clear the slate so I can strain more to prove myself next time. That's law without grace, and it only leads to more slavery, discouragement, pride, and guilt. Grace takes us off the treadmill of always trying to measure up and puts us into a new relationship with a joyful God who gladly welcomes us to be His own. Then, our status changes and our motives are transformed. We begin to want to obey instead of seeing God's commands as burdens. We want to participate in the family business of telling the good news to the world—not to impress anyone, but so more people will be amazed by God's infinite love.

For many years, I was the elder brother in Jesus' story. I heard the sounds of the party for a long time, but I refused to go in and celebrate. Like the obstinate brother, I lived in the Father's presence, but I missed His tender affection. I believed that I had to prove myself to God, to myself, and to everyone who was watching. I insisted on making sure I did enough to impress God . . . and it almost killed me.

Thank God, that wasn't the end for me. God's whispers and shouts finally got my attention. I finally came to the end of myself and reached out to grasp God's loving hand. That was the end, and it was a new beginning. Nothing will ever be the same.

Your worst days are never so bad that you are beyond the reach of God's grace. And your best days are never so good that you are beyond the need of God's grace.

—Jerry Bridges

Consider this . . .

1. In what ways is grace beautiful and attractive? In what ways is it offensive?

2. What are some reasons self-effort to prove ourselves (to God, to ourselves, and to others) feels so right?

3. When the younger brother in Jesus' story came home, how would you describe his motivation to help out at the farm? How is that different from his older brother's motivation to work hard?

4. How would you describe the three purposes of God's laws? What is their relationship to His grace?

5. Has there been a point in your Christian life when you've forgotten grace (see 2 Peter 1:3–9)? If so, how did forgetting God's abundant love affect your mood, your motivation, and your behavior?

6. What would it mean for you to bathe in the grace of God?

7. What is God saying to you in this chapter?

3 ASTONISHED

> Faith is a living, daring confidence in God's grace, so sure and certain that a man could stake his life on it a thousand times.

—Martin Luther

Timothy Henry Gray was a sixty-year-old homeless man who died from exposure to extreme cold under a railroad bridge in Evanston, Wyoming, in 2012. Children who were sledding nearby found his body. For over twenty years, Gray had wandered penniless and alone. When his siblings were found and told about their brother's death, they explained that he was the adopted great-grandson of a United States Senator, who had made a fortune in copper and railroads. The total inheritance for the siblings was about $300 million; Gray's share was about $19 million, but he never claimed a cent of the money. Ironically, he was found under a Union Pacific bridge, the company his ancestor had built and the source of his fortune.[3]

For many years, I was like Timothy Gray. I had inherited the fabulous wealth of God's love, power, and assurance, but I lived like a beggar. The irony of proximity wasn't lost on me: I lived every day with the Word of God, talking about the Spirit of God with the people of God, but I was a pauper. The magnificent blessings of God were already mine, but I didn't possess them and enjoy them.

All the forgiveness, the love, the delight of God, and the power that raised Jesus from the dead are ours now. But many of us live in fear, spiritual and emotional poverty, anxiety, and discouragement because we don't claim what God has already given us.

My Awakening

When I walked away from our prolonged and magnificent staff lunch when we asked, "What if?", I had glimmers of an emotion I hadn't experienced in a long time. It was hope. It was as though I had been wearing blinders for many years, and suddenly, the blinders had been removed. I heard the message of God's love like it was the first time I had heard it—and it thrilled me! I read passages I had read dozens (maybe hundreds) of times before, but this time, I saw grace in every word instead of demands and guilt.

I began to rest in what Jesus had done for me. It felt really odd, but it felt wonderful! For so long, my mind had been running on overdrive trying to figure out the next thing I had to do to make life work and to polish my reputation. Suddenly, my reputation wasn't in question. Rampant, toxic insecurity was washed away like grime in a hot, soapy shower.

A new joy permeated my soul, my words, and my relationships. But there was some repair work to do. Over the next days and weeks, Kim and I had long talks, and for the first time in a long time, I really listened. I asked her to tell me how the last few years of my manic behavior had hurt her. We recounted times when I had barked at her for a mistake at a service—a mistake she had nothing to do with. She had simply been a convenient target for my rage and blame. She told me how I'd hurt

Kyla and Kade by being so distant, so angry, and so demanding. I wasn't defensive. I didn't try to excuse my behavior. I knew it was all true . . . and undoubtedly I had done much more than we recounted. I asked Kim and the kids to forgive me. They were so kind. It was beautiful.

The promises of God became real to me. Before, they had mocked me. I had read and taught passages about peace, but I had no peace at all. The promises of God to bless me were so foreign that I had felt even farther from God—but no longer. I couldn't stop talking about the wonder of God's grace. Our staff had fantastic times talking and praying together. It was better than all of us hitting the lottery . . . far better.

But a few things didn't go so smoothly. The months of being recaptured by grace proved to be some of the most difficult in my ministry. I was excited about experiencing the limitless love of God, but the more I talked about it, the more some people opposed me. I wasn't surprised. I was deeply disappointed that they couldn't see what I was finally seeing, but after all, it had taken me forever to see it. I needed to give them some time and room as well.

However, a few leaders needed more time and room than I thought! Some of them came to me and said, "Ben, if you insist on teaching all this about grace, you'll have to leave the church. We want you to go back to the way things were before you got on your grace kick."

In the past, I would have immediately buckled under. My professional position was my life, and I couldn't bear to lose it. Now, my identity wasn't tied up in my role, my position, or my reputation. It was tied up in the love of Jesus. That mattered more to me than anything else. I responded, "I'm sorry, but I can't go back. That was slavery. It was crushing me, and it made me a terrible leader, husband, and father. No, I'm not going back to the way things were. I can't stop talking about the grace of God. If I have to leave because of this, so be it. But I can't turn my back on the grace, love, and joy I've experienced."

During these difficult conversations, my heart was filled with God's presence and peace. I wasn't afraid of losing my job. If I lost it over the issue of grace, I could live with that. And I wasn't angry with the people who opposed me. I was calm, objective, and rational. (What a concept!) But there were no guarantees.

Perhaps the biggest change was in how I related to our kids. When I was on the performance treadmill, my ego was so fragile that I saw everything my children did as a reflection of me. I treated them like I treated our staff: demanding, blaming, and controlling. When they disobeyed or even made a mistake, I scowled and sent them to their rooms. I snarled, "You'd better pray and read your Bible! And *you* get right with God!"

I cringe when I think about the condemnation I imposed on my children. But now, things were changing. I was there for them in a way I hadn't been for most of their lives. It took them some time to get used to the "new dad," but they liked the new model a lot better than the old one. I spoke far more words of love and affirmation than correction, and when I needed to correct them, it wasn't out of anger but love. I think they liked that difference, too! (I share much more about the restoration of our relationships in chapter 7.)

I had to reframe every way I communicated with the people of our church. I'd tried to motivate them before, but it was manipulative. I told them, "*If* you give and serve, *then* God will bless you." Always if and then, if and then. That's the sound of religion. I realized that was nothing but works-righteousness! God *has already* blessed them, so they can give and serve out of gratitude and joy. I had to learn a new language. Sometimes I slipped and spoke the old language, but I often caught myself in mid-sentence.

For the first time in a long, long time, I
genuinely loved people instead of using
them to prop up my plans.

I sensed the sheer delight of God, and it changed me. For the first time in a long, long time, I genuinely loved people instead of using them to prop up my plans. I relaxed and enjoyed the ministry. Instead of feeling like I had to make it successful, I realized I had a front row seat to watch the Spirit of God work in magnificent ways to change lives. Now, I loved working with people and serving God!

As I shared what God was teaching me, many others in every walk of life told me how grace was revolutionizing their lives. Young and old, rich and poor, the down-and-outers and the up-and-comers, people of every color and stripe were being set free and energized by the grace of God. It was infectious . . . in a really good way.

The Heart of the Gospel

A friend of mine asked a small group he was leading, "Do you think God grades on a curve?"

One of the men in the group blurted out, "I sure hope so!"

My friend waited a second and then explained, "Actually, He *doesn't* grade on a curve. He demands perfection, and we don't meet it—on our own." This brief exchange led to a wonderful conversation about the true meaning of the gospel of Jesus Christ.

Like the man who hoped God grades on a curve, many people sitting in churches today believe they're pretty good people, and the gospel gives them a little help "over the hump" to be a little better so God will accept them. The message of the Bible, from the first page to the last, is that this concept couldn't be further from the truth!

Part of the problem is that western people who are products of the Enlightenment believe we are, at heart, noble people. Sure, we mess up at times, but we're essentially good. Christians have been affected by this thinking. We wouldn't agree with the teaching of philosophers like Rousseau, but Rousseau's teaching about the goodness of humanity has still made us wonder how bad we really are. After all, we haven't committed mass murder, we aren't members of the mob, and we don't sell drugs to kids on the black market. Compared to people who do those things, we conclude we're not too bad.

Yes, compared to them, that's true. But the Bible compares us to someone else: the holy, unapproachably righteous God of glory! In Paul's most extensive treatment of humanity's condition, God's holiness, and the meaning of the gospel, he goes to great lengths to show us that we fall short—infinitely short—of God's standards. He explained, "For all have sinned and fall short of the glory of God" (Rom. 3:23), we are powerless to impress God (Rom. 5:6), and in fact, we have made ourselves His enemies (Rom. 5:10).

The power of this indictment is God's law. The Ten Commandments, the 600 or so various commands in the Old Testament, and the even stricter requirements in the New Testament should make us tremble! We don't measure up, and in fact, we can't measure up! God's perfect law reveals our sins, and in fact incites our sins, because we naturally rebel against God.

In his letter to the Ephesians, Paul explains that we aren't close to getting right with God through our own efforts. We are helpless and hopeless! We are "dead in [our] transgressions," deserving God's righteous wrath (Eph. 2:1–3).

We were married to the law, but our harsh spouse condemned us at every moment. Why? Because we were guilty! God's holy, righteous law isn't the problem. The problem is our sin—compared to God. This includes the sins of even the most noble among us. Something or someone had to die to set us free. God's solution wasn't meek and mild. It was drastic and dramatic. The righteous judgment of a holy God was that we deserved His eternal wrath. We deserved to die. The message of the gospel is that God stepped out of heaven to pay the price for us. Jesus paid the debt we couldn't pay by dying the death we deserved to die.

Why in the world would God do something so magnificently wonderful for helpless, hopeless, rebellious enemies? There's only one answer: He loves us. After Paul described our desperate, hopeless condition apart from God, he wrote a beautiful conjunction: *but*. This word completely changes the trajectory of our destinies:

> But because of his great love for us, God, who is rich in mercy, made us alive with Christ, even when we were dead in transgressions—it is by grace you have been saved. . . . in order that in the coming ages he might show the incomparable riches of his grace, expressed in his kindness to us in Christ Jesus. (Eph. 2:4–7)

When Jesus died on the cross, He didn't just come to die *for* Ben Dailey; He died *as* Ben Dailey. He took all my sins, and the sins of every person who ever lived or will live, and took our place of punishment. As I thought more accurately about the gospel, I saw depressed Ben Dailey on the cross as Jesus died, I saw bitter Ben Dailey, controlling Ben Dailey, anxious Ben Dailey, self-important Ben Dailey, enraged Ben Dailey, terrified

Ben Dailey. That's the Ben Dailey who was caught up in the person of Jesus Christ, and He died as me.

The old Ben Dailey died on the cross with Jesus, but a new Ben Dailey was raised to new life through the resurrection. That's why Paul could say, "I have been crucified with Christ; and it is no longer I who live, but Christ lives in me; and the life which I now live in the flesh I live by faith in the Son of God, who loved me and gave Himself up for me." But Paul wasn't finished with his thought. He drew a line in the sand so we wouldn't miss the centrality of the sacrifice of Christ. If we try to prove ourselves, to impress God and people, we remain under the penalty of the law, and the sacrifice of Jesus means nothing to us. Paul explained, "I do not nullify the grace of God, for if righteousness comes through the Law, then Christ died needlessly" (Gal. 2:20–21, NASB). That should stop us in our tracks: When we think, believe, and act like we can do enough to impress God with our goodness and obedience, we're actually saying that Christ died for nothing!

I had been married to the law. I tried like crazy to please my spouse, but it was never enough. All I got were scowls, condemnation, and reminders that I was never good enough. When the old Ben died, the new one had a new husband: Jesus Christ. What is this husband like? He's full of kindness, tenderness, joy, delight, and affection. I had always secretly thought God was angry with me. I was so wrong. The law, my old husband, was a stern taskmaster, but God was never against me.

Changing spouses radically changes our motivations. Paul extends his explanation of the impact of this change by explaining that death has released us from the penalty of the law so we can enjoy the life of the Spirit:

So, my brothers and sisters, you also died to the law through the body of Christ, that you might belong to another, to him who was raised from the dead, in order that we might bear fruit for God. For when we were in the realm of the flesh, the sinful passions aroused by the law were at work in us, so that we bore fruit for death. But now, by dying to what once bound us, we have been released from the law so that we serve in the new way of the Spirit, and not in the old way of the written code. (Rom. 7:4–6)

When I looked back on all those lost years of grueling drudgery, I realized God had been whispering and shouting to get my attention and remind me of His love, but I had missed it. I never want to miss it again! God is a lover, not a torturer. He smiles; He doesn't scowl. This revelation was an incredible relief to me. The burden of not measuring up, feeling condemned all day every day was finally gone—not because I found some way to be more successful, more controlling, and more impressive, but because I finally gave up on all that and found the beautiful love of Jesus.

Life is so different when we're married to Jesus. He always acts in grace and truth, never with condemnation and anger. He wants one thing above all from us: to eagerly receive His love and let it melt and mold us from the inside out. He constantly reminds us of His love, empowers us to do whatever He asks us to do, assures us that we can't slip from His arms, and promises an eternal honeymoon in the new heaven and new earth.

The problem isn't God's magnificent grace; the problem is our ability to grasp the enormous extent of His great love. Old messages drown out God's sweet voice, and old habits of proving ourselves still promise fulfillment. Until we're convinced—in the depths of our souls—that we've died to the law and been raised to a new life with a new spouse, we'll keep leaning back toward the old, familiar, performance-driven life.

We'll try to meet standards we can't meet, and we'll fail again and again. We'll address this problem in detail in chapters 5 and 6, but for now, don't be shocked if the wonder of this new relationship with God sometimes grows dim. For many of us, it is literally too good to be true. Sooner or later, we need to be overwhelmed with grace so that we are utterly astonished by our new identity (who we are) and our new relationship with God (whose we are). Both are essential elements of a new life of grace.

Sooner or later, we need to be overwhelmed with grace so that we are utterly astonished by our new identity (who we are) and our new relationship with God (whose we are).

Justified

When we believe our sins are forgiven only up to the point of salvation and then we have to crank out obedience on our own, we miss the joy and power of the Christian life. A term that Paul uses often in Romans is "justified." The law, the righteous commandments of God, can only condemn us, but they point to someone who did fulfill them. Paul explained, "But now apart from the law the righteousness of God has been made known, to which the Law and the Prophets testify" (Rom. 3:21). What do the Law and the Prophets tell us? "This righteousness is given through faith in Jesus Christ to all who believe. There is no difference between Jew and Gentile, for all have sinned and fall short of the glory of God, and all are justified freely by his grace through the redemption that came by Christ Jesus" (Rom. 3:22–24). Let's look at some of the many gifts God gives us when He justifies us.

Complete Forgiveness: Many church leaders use an old Sunday school phrase to explain justification. They say it means "just as if I'd never sinned." That's fairly helpful, but it's only part of the truth. There are actually two aspects to this central concept. First, it means that Jesus paid an infinite price for our infinite debt. There is no way we can pay for it—the debt is too big and our efforts are too flawed. Perfect law required a perfect sacrifice—the atoning death of the perfect Son of God. It's not just that our past sins are forgiven. All of our sins, even those we haven't committed yet, were completely paid for on the cross of Christ. It actually *is* finished! Paul assures us, "Therefore, there is now no condemnation for those who are in Christ Jesus" (Rom. 8:1).

Counted Righteous: The second aspect of justification is often overlooked. As Paul explained, sin has been taken away through the death of Christ, and His righteousness has been imputed to us. This isn't just a concept. When Jesus lived on earth, He perfectly and completely obeyed the Father. He loved God with all His heart, soul, and mind, and He loved His neighbor as Himself. When we trust in Christ, God imputes Jesus' perfect righteousness to our account. We didn't earn it, and in this life we don't live up to it. This status is the free, amazing gift of God.

We aren't the first to be counted righteous. Paul reminds us that our ancestor in the faith, Abraham, "believed God, and it was credited to him as righteousness" (Rom. 4:3 and Gen. 15:6). Paul knew human nature. He was well aware that we'd try to take credit for our new status, so he put us in our place by reminding us that self-effort can't earn anything with God. From first to last, grace comes only by faith. He wrote, "Now to the one who works, wages are not credited as a gift but as an obligation. However, to the one who does not work but trusts

God who justifies the ungodly, their faith is credited as righteousness" (Rom. 4:4–5).

A single change in a preposition changed my life. For years, I focused on what I did *for* Christ. Legalism promises success by self-effort, but it drains our lives away. It was all about duty, obligation, and demands, and it led to emptiness, self-absorption, competition, and condemnation. Then I began to be amazed at who I was *in* Christ—totally forgiven, fully accepted, deeply loved, and counted as righteous as Jesus! I was thrilled, overwhelmed, and humbled. I still am, and even more as I continue to understand the gospel more deeply.

Paul describes our new condition as being "in Christ." That means His status of sonship becomes our status and His righteousness is counted as ours. To the believers in Paul's day, it was a revolutionary new concept. He used the word *mystery* to mean God's truth that had been hidden but was now revealed. He wrote the Colossians about "the mystery that has been kept hidden for ages and generations, but is now disclosed to the Lord's people. To them God has chosen to make known among the Gentiles the glorious riches of this mystery, which is Christ in you, the hope of glory" (Col. 1:26–27).

This two-letter preposition isn't an abstract theological concept. It transformed my entire understanding of the Christian life! I had been working, trying, controlling, and worrying. I thought I had to do enough to earn God's favor, but no matter how much I did, it was never enough. Being in Christ—as loved by the Father as Jesus and counted as righteous as Jesus—brought me something I hadn't experienced in years: a deep, wonderful sense of peace.

Access and Intimacy: As I drew closer to God, I realized I used to have a business relationship with God. I made deals (or I

tried to make deals) with Him: "God, I'll do this if you'll do that."
I assumed I could get leverage over Him if I just did enough. In
Free of Charge, Miroslav Volf observes that a common miscon-
ception of God is treating Him as "a negotiator." Volf shows
the logical end of this view: If we see God as a negotiator, we're
immediately at a disadvantage because He has already placed
incredibly high demands on us—demands no one can keep. "If
God is a negotiator, what happens if we break the deal we've
made? . . . God the negotiator inescapably turns into God the
judge."[4] We have a choice: If we have a business relationship
with God and try to make deals with Him, He always becomes
a fierce, condemning judge to us. But if we see Him as a God of
infinite goodness and grace, we'll gladly receive His gifts and be
transformed by His kindness.

The idea of being justified in the sight of God isn't a sterile
thing. As I delved more deeply into the wonder of grace and
my justification, I realized I have open access to the Father. I
don't have to fear Him any longer, and I'm not angry with Him
because I think He let me down. The mighty King has become
my Father! And He invites me to be with Him, to talk with Him,
and to delight in His love. He longs for me to "approach [His]
throne of grace with confidence" that He cares, He hears, and
He always has my best interests in mind (Heb. 4:16).

As I pray, as I drive to work, as I meet with people, and in a
hundred other things I do each day, I often think of the awesome
fact that I can always approach the God of the universe. My
Father wants me to be with Him. Heaven's doors have been
opened to me! My circumstances may not be any different, but
my connection with God brings me favor, blessing, assurance,
and peace—no matter how good or bad my situation may be.

Amazing Freedom: God doesn't just offer us a bare taste
of freedom from condemnation, guilt, and the oppressive burden

of always trying to measure up but always falling short. He commands us to bathe in this freedom! The Galatian Christians tried to go back to the law instead of enjoying the grace of God. Their leaders taught people they had to follow the commands of the Old Testament to be right with God. Paul wasn't diplomatic or polite in his response to them. He wrote,

> You foolish Galatians! Who has bewitched you? Before your very eyes Jesus Christ was clearly portrayed as crucified. I would like to learn just one thing from you: Did you receive the Spirit by the works of the law, or by believing what you heard? Are you so foolish? After beginning by means of the Spirit, are you now trying to finish by means of the flesh? Have you experienced so much in vain—if it really was in vain? (Gal. 3:1–4)

Trying to live by the law isn't Christian, and it isn't the gospel. It's the opposite of the gospel, and it's against Christ! Paul drew a stark contrast between slavery to self-effort and the law and freedom in Christ:

> It is for freedom that Christ has set us free. Stand firm, then, and do not let yourselves be burdened again by a yoke of slavery. . . . You who are trying to be justified by the law have been alienated from Christ; you have fallen away from grace. For through the Spirit we eagerly await by faith the righteousness for which we hope. (Gal. 5:1, 4–5)

We are so free in Christ's love and power that Paul wrote that "all things are lawful for me, but not all things are helpful. All things are lawful for me, but I will not be dominated by anything" (1 Cor. 6:12, ESV). The incredible freedom we have in Christ is always tempered and directed by love for those around us.

The incredible freedom we have in Christ is always tempered and directed by love for those around us.

A Radically New Motivation: This kind of freedom scares a lot of people. They assume people will take the liberty to sin all they want! They don't understand that immeasurable love produces incredible freedom that always produces a new desire to please the One who sets us free. In the first century, some others obviously made the same erroneous assumption that grace opens the door to sin, and in fact, promotes sin.

In his letter to the Romans, Paul clearly and boldly blasted the error. He posed the question and then answered it with a question of his own: "What shall we say, then? Shall we go on sinning so that grace may increase? By no means! We are those who have died to sin; how can we live in it any longer?" (Rom. 6:1–2) In other words, Paul says the argument that grace leads to sin simply doesn't make any sense. Grace isn't just a warm fuzzy feeling. It's God's dramatic act to identify us with the payment for sin by the death of Jesus, and then identify us with the new life of the resurrected Jesus. We now live in a new kingdom, with a new King and spouse, a new purpose, and new heart. Everything has changed, especially our identity and our motivations. If we have even an inkling of what grace means, we'll want to please God with every fiber of our being!

As I experienced more freedom through the gospel of grace, something happened deep in the machinery of my heart. Some cogs slipped into a different gear. Suddenly, I didn't try to see how much I could get away with before I got caught, and I didn't try to see how close I could get to sin without actually sinning. I suddenly wanted to honor God, to delight Him, to be more like Him, and to represent Him to the people around me. Grace produced a freedom that energized a new motivation for obedience.

Grace seems like the easiest concept in the world to grasp, but in fact, it's one of the hardest. Our natural inclination is to see God as a harsh negotiator or judge. When we realize He genuinely and truly loves us, some people have another distorted view: they see Him as a celestial Santa Claus. They sit passively waiting for God to do everything for them. But grace actually gives us a new energy, a new power to be the people God wants us to be and do the things He wants us to do. Paul certainly understood and experienced this dynamic. Luke's account of Paul's journeys showed the way God's grace gave Paul direction, tenacity, and strength to spread the kingdom of Christ around the known world. He explained this power to the Colossians: "He is the one we proclaim, admonishing and teaching everyone with all wisdom, so that we may present everyone fully mature in Christ. To this end I strenuously contend with all the energy Christ so powerfully works in me" (Col. 1:28–29). The grace of God gave Paul—and it gives us—a wonderful blend of peace and intensity about the right things, rest from self-effort, and tenacity to do anything and everything to honor God.

Family Affection: Before the revelation of God's grace hit me like a freight train, I had seen Kim, Kyla, and Kade as an extension of my reputation. I don't think I ever said it, but I'm quite sure they understood that their main goal in life was to make me look good. When they did, I took them for granted. When they didn't, I let them know it. It was sick.

I treated our staff the same way. They were pawns on the huge chessboard of my career. In a thousand different ways, verbally and nonverbally, I let them know their value was based on how they advanced my career. It was offensive.

I was very polite and kind to the people in our church, but it was all image management. I was selling a product: me, and I hoped they would buy it by coming, giving, and participating. It was a game.

All of my relationships were shaped by my radical insecurity. I didn't feel loved, so I had no love to give. I didn't feel accepted, so I didn't accept others warmly. I wasn't convinced I was forgiven, so I didn't forgive people for their flaws (and I found plenty that weren't even there). I tried to be the center of the universe for all the people around me, but my compulsion to control them left me isolated and left them confused.

Grace began to transform every connection in my life. As my heart was filled and overflowing with the love of God, I gradually stopped blaming, manipulating, and using people for my ends. Instead of competing with them, I affirm them as loved and valuable people, and I appreciate their contributions to the kingdom. Instead of finding fault with anything they do, I'm more aware of how God no longer finds fault with me. Today, I rejoice when they succeed, and I feel genuine compassion for them when they suffer. That's different, completely different.

Grace means that we accept the person, but not always the behavior. I've heard people say they "want to extend grace" to an alcoholic or a liar or a thief or some other person (often a family member) by not speaking the truth or holding the person accountable. That's not love; that's cowardice. God loves us so much that He speaks the hard truth to us and corrects us with discipline—but always in love, not wrath, and always for our good.

The writer to the Hebrews shows us how God's love leads Him to correct us:

> Endure hardship as disciplines; God is treating you as his children. For what children are not disciplined by their father? If you are not disciplined—and everyone undergoes discipline—then you are not legitimate, not true sons and daughters at all. Moreover, we have all had human fathers who disciplined us and we respected them for it. How much more should we submit to the Father of spirits and live! (Heb. 12:7–9)

Our relationships with each other, then, can reflect the way God relates to us when we need correction. If we love them, we speak the truth to them and call them to turn back to God. Paul instructed, "Brothers and sisters, if someone is caught in a sin, you who live by the Spirit should restore that person gently. But watch yourselves, or you also may be tempted. Carry each other's burdens, and in this way you will fulfill the law of Christ" (Gal. 6:1–2).

"Speaking the truth in love" (Eph. 4:15) covers the full range of grace-filled communication: affirmation, encouragement, support, questions, correction, and restoration. It's always focused on building up the other person instead of tearing them down.

Parents and leaders in business and the church can let grace direct their relationships. I used to manipulate people to achieve my own ends of power and prestige, but now I want to convince people that the grace of God can set them free to be all God wants them to be. When I need to correct, I do it for their sake, for their good, and their futures, not so they'll conform to my standards to make me look good. (At least, that's what I'm learning to do.)

Nothing Deeper

I've heard some people complain, "That grace stuff is good for people who are unbelievers to get them into the kingdom, and maybe for new believers to get them started well, but those of us who are more mature in our faith need to move on to deeper things." That's so wrong! When we read the pages of the Bible, we realize there's nothing deeper than God's grace. It points us to the majesty of God, who in His sovereign power and kindness had a plan to redeem lost people. Grace shows us the limitless love of God. We were His enemies; we had nothing to offer Him. And besides, He needed nothing, but He gave His only Son. Grace isn't just a doctrine; it's embodied in a person. We don't just read about it in dusty theological texts. We see it in the face of Jesus, we hear it in the voice of Jesus, and we sense it in the presence of Jesus.

The writer to the Hebrews tells us that spiritual milk is for baby Christians, but solid food is for the mature. Jesus is the first milk a person needs, and it satisfies, and He is the meat that gives ultimate sustenance. We can paddle in grace like a child in a puddle, and we can dive into it like a submarine going to the deepest ocean depths. It amazes the new believer, and it amazes the greatest theologians. The Hebrews' writer makes sure we don't miss Jesus. After recounting all the stories of great men and women of faith, he points us to the source:

> Therefore, since we are surrounded by such a great cloud of witnesses, let us throw off everything that hinders and the sin that so easily entangles. And let us run with perseverance the race marked out for us,

fixing our eyes on Jesus, the pioneer and perfecter of faith. For the joy set before him he endured the cross, scorning its shame, and sat down at the right hand of the throne of God. (Heb. 12:1–2)

What was "the joy set before him"? What propelled Jesus to endure torture, ridicule, and separation from the Father so He could endure hell? It was you. It was me. He anticipated the joy of having us as His own, of setting us free to love Him supremely and follow Him joyfully. We'll never get to the bottom of His limitless love.

Christianity isn't a sin management program.

Christianity isn't a sin management program. Jesus didn't say, "I came that you might have rules and religion." He came that we might have an abundant life filled with knowing and loving Him, amazed at the wonder of His majesty and affection, humbled that He would give Himself for sinners like us, and inspired by a new sense of purpose to honor Him in everything we do.

Karl Marx famously stated, "Religion is the opiate of the people." Many believers have been incensed by his critique of religion, but he's right: Mankind's penchant for self-validation, self-justification, and self-improvement through religious practices doesn't make us fully alive—these pursuits deaden our hearts and leave us spiritually numb. Many of us who call ourselves Christians have got it wrong. Robert Farrar Capon, author of many insightful books on God's grace, observed that many of us have become little more than bookkeepers. In *The Parables of Grace*, Capon wrote,

Jesus has already been critical of the following items taken from everybody's list of Favorite Things to Be: Being First, Being Found, Being Big, Being Important, and Being Alive. Now however, he castigates the one item that holds all these futilities together and gives them power over us, namely, Being a Bookkeeper. The human race is positively addicted to keeping records and remembering scores. What we call our "life" is, for the most part, simply the juggling of accounts in our heads. And yet, if God has announced anything in Jesus, it is that He, for one, has pensioned off the book-keeping department permanently. . . . It may be our sacred conviction that the only way to keep God happy, the stars in their courses, our children safe, our psyches adjusted, and our neighbors reasonable is to be ready, at every moment, to have the books we have kept on ourselves and others audited. But that is not God's conviction because he has taken away the handwriting that was against us (Col. 2:14).[5]

Bookkeeping never melts a person's hard heart or thrills a soul. Only grace can do that. People who experience the grace of God never get over the wonder of it. Sadly, the church can exist for many years without grasping the truth and beauty of God's limitless love. Five centuries ago, Martin Luther and a group of believers had a revelation of grace. The church had been teaching that people had to jump through hoops to earn God's acceptance and pay for forgiveness with their contributions. Luther began to study the Bible, particularly Paul's letters to the Galatians and the Romans, and his teaching turned the world upside down. The wonder of God's grace stunned and amazed Luther and many others in his day.

Grace still amazes us . . . if we can only let God convince us it's true.

People who insist on negotiating deals with God and try to impress Him with all their efforts see Jesus as only an example to follow. They try to "be like Jesus" and do all the things "good Christians" do, but not with delight and gratitude. Certainly, Jesus is an example . . . the very best example, but if that's all He is, trying to live up to His perfection will crush us into the dust. A few years ago, it was all the rage to wear bracelets that read, "WWJD," What would Jesus do? It implied that if we just took a second to think, we could realize what Jesus would do in any situation and do it. Here's a news flash: We can't do what Jesus did in the first century, and we can't do what Jesus can still do today. We can't approach the integrity, compassion, and self-lessness of Christ. Jesus did precisely what none of us could do: He pleased the Father perfectly.

Someone said, "You just need to follow Jesus' instructions in the Sermon on the Mount. That's the way to live." Well, sure. Just try it. Go out and be light and salt, bless those who insult you and persecute you, never lust, never get angry, never want revenge, love your enemies, have pure motives, don't worry about problems, don't harshly judge others, and bear genuine fruit in all you do. I think any objective reader would finish the sermon and say, "Oh my, I can't possibly live this way!" Precisely. Jesus' standards are even higher than the laws in the Old Testament. No one could obey them, and no one can obey the higher ones in the Sermon on the Mount. We fall short . . . way short. That's why we need a Savior.

Jesus isn't a means to our ends of self-validation and self-glory. He is the end, and if we trust Him, He is all we want or need. He's first our Savior, our Friend, our Brother, and if we really know Him, He is our tender, strong, loving Husband. Our lives are no longer about duty to obey, but about being filled with wonder at the beauty of God. He becomes the object of our delight. King David wrote,

> One thing I have asked from the LORD, that I shall seek:
> That I may dwell in the house of the LORD all the days
>   of my life,
> To behold the beauty of the LORD
> And to meditate in His temple. (Ps. 27:4, NASB)

Is the Lord beautiful to you? He can be, but not by trying harder to be a good person.

After that afternoon in the restaurant with our staff, I became astonished at the grace of God poured out to me, for me, and in me. It has changed me. Grace shattered me, and it rebuilt me. I'm less fragile and more honest about my flaws, less demanding and more grateful, less disillusioned and more optimistic that belonging to God is the greatest adventure known to mankind.

I hope you'll be astonished, too.

We've looked at a lot of Scriptures in this chapter, but that's okay. I wanted you to see that the message of grace is on every page of the Bible you've been reading for years. It's there, it's clear, and it's been there all along.

The meaning of life. The wasted years of life. The poor choices of life. God answers the mess of life with one word: grace.

—Max Lucado

Consider this . . .

1. How does it affect people to believe that the sacrifice of Christ covers only the sins they committed *before* they trusted Him? What do they do about their sins after that?

2. What is the importance of the second aspect of justification, the righteousness of Christ imputed to us?

3. How might a clearer, more expansive view of Jesus and His grace affect a person's prayer life?

4. Describe how the freedom of a grace-filled life revolution-
   izes our motivation to obey God and follow His commands.

5. Which specific changes described in this chapter (or others
   you've thought of as you read it) have you experienced as
   you've trusted in the grace of God? (Or which ones are
   most attractive to you?)

6. Is the Lord beautiful to you? Explain your answer.

7. What is God saying to you in this chapter?

4 TREASURE TIMES TWO

> ❝ It is not the strength of your faith that saves you,
> but the strength of Him upon whom you rely. ❞
>
> **—Charles Spurgeon**

On July 20, 1985, Mel Fisher stood on the deck of his salvage boat off the Florida Keys. He had been searching for seventeen years for the wreck of the Atocha, a Spanish galleon that sank in a hurricane in 1622. The archives of the ship's manifest listed quantities of gold, silver, and emeralds that amounted to a king's ransom. In fact, when the ship sank, the Spanish economy suffered a financial depression. (I can imagine the king was depressed, too!)

Early in the search, Fisher had found a few pieces of the treasure that tantalized him and his crew. However, tragedy struck in 1975 when one of the salvage boats capsized in a storm, and Fisher's son and two other divers were killed. Over the years, funding for the treasure hunt often ran out, and Fisher had to bring on more investors to keep the operation going. The investors were lured by the tangible evidence of a few coins here, a bracelet there, a cannon that was unmistakably from the Atocha . . . and the promise of incredible riches if they ever found the main treasure. Nothing, it seemed, could stop Mel Fisher from his quest. He kept going through the deaths of his son and two crew members, financial hardship, and the taunts of those who thought he was crazy to look so long and find so little.

On the hot summer day in July of 1985, Fisher was using a new technique to blow the white sand off the bottom of the ocean floor to uncover anything buried there. As he had done on countless days over seventeen years, he watched the bubbles from the air tanks of his divers when they went down to see if anything appeared when the sand was removed. And as he had done all those days, he waited and hoped. Suddenly, one of the divers came to the surface, ripped his regulator out of his mouth and yelled, "It's here! We've found the main pile!"

Through the gradually clearing water, the divers had seen an incredible sight: a stack of gold and silver bars eight feet wide, four feet high and twenty feet long! All around the stack were gold candelabra, embossed gold platters, bracelets and chains. There were piles of emeralds, many of them huge. The recovery operation took months. In all, the treasure was valued at over $400 million. On July nineteenth, people said Mel Fisher was a fool. On the afternoon of the twentieth, they said he was a genius—a rich genius. He had found a fabulous treasure!

Jesus Is Our Treasure

Jesus told two short parables with a similar message:

> "The kingdom of heaven is like treasure hidden in a field. When a man found it, he hid it again, and then in his joy went and sold all he had and bought that field. Again, the kingdom of heaven is like a merchant looking for fine pearls. When he found one of great value, he went away and sold everything he had and bought it." (Matt. 13:44–46)

Jesus compared the kingdom of heaven with a man who found a treasure in a field. The ancient Middle East was the site of many battles as armies moved from Mesopotamia to Egypt and back again. When an army approached, people tried to save their valuables by burying them. Sometimes, the people were killed or captured and displaced, and the treasure remained buried for decades until the rain washed the dirt away and somebody found it. That's the scene here. The man who found the treasure evidently wasn't looking for it (though in the following story, the pearl merchant was looking for an exceptionally valuable pearl). The man simply stumbled upon the treasure. We can imagine him noticing a corner of a buried box, lifting it out, and brushing the dirt off the top. When he opened it, he found it to be more valuable than anything he could imagine, so he buried it again and sold all he had to buy the field so the treasure could be his. The treasure meant more to him than anything in the world.

The treasure in the field symbolizes Christ. Some of us, like the pearl merchant, look diligently for God, but many others stumble upon Christ in the course of our normal lives. If we grasp how wonderful He is, how unspeakably great and kind, how infinitely powerful and loving—and that He loves us personally—we, like the man in the parable, joyfully give up everything we have so we can enjoy this treasure. Don't misunderstand the message here. Jesus wasn't teaching that we can do anything to "buy" His love or our salvation. No, this parable teaches that the treasure of knowing Christ is so rich and wonderful that nothing, absolutely nothing, compares with it.

Paul captured the heart of this concept in his letter to the Philippians. He recounted all of his accomplishments and his credentials. He was a rising leader in the Jewish religion, a lion of a leader who was respected (and feared) by all. Through his intelligence, determination, and skill, he was rising to the top of his society. Then he met Jesus, and his world turned upside down. Suddenly, the power and prestige he had pursued seemed meaningless—actually, less than meaningless, they were like garbage, even dung. They had become repulsive to Paul. He explained his new perspective and his new treasure:

> But whatever were gains to me I now consider loss for the sake of Christ. What is more, I consider everything a loss because of the surpassing worth of knowing Christ Jesus my Lord, for whose sake I have lost all things. I consider them garbage, that I may gain Christ and be found in him, not having a righteousness of my own that comes from the law, but that which is through faith in Christ—the righteousness that comes from God on the basis of faith. I want to know Christ. (Phil. 3:7–10)

When Mel Fisher looked at the incredible treasure of gold, silver, and emeralds, he didn't shrug his shoulders and think, *Big deal*. He was amazed, thrilled, and excited! If we don't understand the fabulous treasure Jesus is to us, we treat Him like a tool or an employee, someone to help us accomplish our goals. Author and psychologist Larry Crabb observes that many of us think of God as "a specially attentive waiter."[6] When we get good service from Him, we give Him a nice tip of praise. When we don't get what we want, we complain.

Jesus isn't our waiter; He's our King and Savior! He's the greatest treasure because of His amazing greatness and His grace. John gives us a glimpse of the majesty of the risen Christ in his vision in the opening chapter of Revelation. Imagine this sight:

> I turned around to see the voice that was speaking to me. And when I turned I saw seven golden lampstands,

and among the lampstands was someone like a son of man, dressed in a robe reaching down to his feet and with a golden sash around his chest. The hair on his head was white like wool, as white as snow, and his eyes were like blazing fire. His feet were like bronze glowing in a furnace, and his voice was like the sound of rushing waters. In his right hand he held seven stars, and coming out of his mouth was a sharp, dou-ble-edged sword. His face was like the sun shining in all its brilliance. (Rev. 1:12–16)

John didn't shrug his shoulders and think, *So what.* He described his response to the greatness of the resurrected Christ:

When I saw him, I fell at his feet as though dead. Then he placed his right hand on me and said: "Do not be afraid. I am the First and the Last. I am the Living One; I was dead, and now look, I am alive for ever and ever! And I hold the keys of death and Hades." (Rev. 1:17–18)

The awesome One is the tender One. The majestic One is the compassionate One. The One who is far above all reaches down to touch, to heal, and to love.

When Jesus stepped out of heaven, He didn't just forfeit some comforts; He laid aside His glory to become one of us. He didn't just risk His reputation; He gave His life for us. When He was arrested, He told those standing near Him that He could instantly call "more than twelve legions of angels" to protect Him (Matt. 26:53). Angels aren't the cute, cuddly, plump little toddlers we see on Valentine's cards. They are so powerful that every person who saw them had to be reassured they wouldn't be immediately turned into ashes! But Jesus didn't call the army of angels to wipe out the human race—which is exactly what we deserved (Matt. 26:53). Instead, as He was dying an excruciating death at the hands of Roman and religious collaborators, He looked down from the cross and prayed, "Father, forgive them, for they do not know what they are doing" (Luke 23:34).

It's absurd to think that we can merit His approval by our striving. In fact, it's insulting to Him and His sacrifice.

When we begin to get a glimpse of Jesus (and even those who have been in church for years may need to get a new glimpse of His power, love, and beauty), we are amazed. The King of glory lived in the splendor of heaven and needed nothing, but He gave everything—for you and me. It's absurd to think that we can merit His approval by our striving. In fact, it's insulting to Him and His sacrifice. Instead, we don't look at our efforts at all.

In the Old Testament, people brought unblemished lambs to the priest to be sacrificed as payment for their sins. When the priest put his hand on the lamb, he carefully examined the lamb to see if it was suitable as a sacrifice—he didn't examine the man or woman who brought it. The question wasn't the person's sin. That was taken for granted. The question was about the validity, the purity, and the perfection of the lamb. Jesus is the perfect, spotless, unblemished Lamb "who takes away the sins of the world" (John 1:29).

In Jesus, infinite power and infinite love are perfectly and completely intertwined. He is the treasure who is a source of wonder to us—in this life and in the one to come.

We Are Christ's Treasure

God isn't angry with us. He doesn't despise us. He's not a surly teacher who enjoys pointing out our ignorance and flaws. He delights in us. He considers us His treasure! An object's worth is based on the price tag. The price God was willing to pay for us was the infinitely valuable life of His Son. To God, we are worth more than the stars in the sky, and all the jewels, gold, oil, and real estate on earth. We marvel at fabulously wealthy people. We can marvel even more because God considers Himself rich because He has us!

Is this conclusion wrong, off-base, maybe even heretical? Doesn't the Bible say God pours out His righteous wrath against sin? Yes, that's the point. We deserved His wrath, but He poured it all out on Jesus to clear the way so He can shower us with His love, blessings, and kindness.

Some of us think God has abandoned us. Life hasn't turned out the way we hoped, and we assume God has gone to another part of the universe—or at least, that's the way it feels. He never leaves us or forsakes us. He assured the people of Israel, and He assures us:

> "Can a mother forget the baby at her breast
> and have no compassion on the child she has borne?
> Though she may forget,
> I will not forget you!
> See, I have engraved you on the palms of my hands."
> (Isa. 49:15–16)

Peter assures us that we are "precious" to God. How precious? He explains:

> But you are a chosen people, a royal priesthood, a holy
> nation, God's special possession, that you may declare

the praises of him who called you out of darkness into his wonderful light. Once you were not a people, but now you are the people of God; once you had not received mercy, but now you have received mercy. (1 Peter 2:9–10)

The word translated "special possession" actually means "treasure" (see Ex. 19:5). God has chosen us, He has given us royal status as His children, and we are part of the vast kingdom of God from every tribe, tongue, and nation. He considers us His "special possession," an object of affection and joy to Him.

Does this truth seem too good to be true? Does your soul recoil from embracing it because it's too wonderful to imagine? Or do you resist because it takes away your pride of accomplishment? If we have any sense of how the grace of God has transformed our identity and destiny, we'll shout like Paul at the end of his explanation to the Roman believers of the wonder of the gospel:

Oh, the depth of the riches of the wisdom and
    knowledge of God!
How unsearchable his judgments,
and his paths beyond tracing out! (Rom. 11:33)

A Revolutionary New Identity

People get their sense of identity from all kinds of sources: their accomplishments, their jobs, the cars they drive, the person they married, the size of their bank accounts, the power they wield, their clothes, their body shape, their degrees, their wit, their political affiliations and a hundred other ways we try to impress those who are watching. On Thursday nights, I run with some friends, and we often run through a part of the city where there are lots of clubs. Each club tries to be unique—hip hop, country, jazz, R&B, you name it—and the people inside may dress differently, but the look on their faces is exactly the same. All of them are trying to impress the people sitting at their table (or maybe the ones sitting at the next table).

Having an identity isn't optional. We have to have one, one we create or one granted to us. Most of us are on a never-ending search to find an identity that fills our hearts and gives us the meaning we long for. Sadly, many people in our churches are no different from the ones at the clubs. We also try to get our identity from what we do. Our list of activities is very different from the people in the bars, but it's a list of behaviors we trust will finally make us somebody. And indeed, they shape us at the deepest level: they make us fearful or arrogant, driven or depressed.

The legalistic message of the church is driving people away. Today, I don't think people are leaving the church because they're leaving Jesus. They're leaving the church because the church has left Jesus.

The problem isn't God's message; the problem is in *not understanding* the clear message of the Bible. From Genesis to Revelation, we find the arc of Scripture: creation, the fall into sin, the story of redemption by grace, and the ultimate restoration. These aren't weighted equally in the text. The first two, creation and fall, are found in the first three chapters of Genesis, and the last one is in the last chapters of Revelation. All the rest of the Bible is a rich, varied, beautiful story of God reaching into our darkness to shine the light of the gospel of grace. If we look carefully, we'll find that the whole Bible is about the beauty, the love, and the sacrifice of Jesus.

When Jesus walked with the two men on the road to Emmaus after the crucifixion, they were confused. They assumed Jesus was going to overthrow the Romans and become the Jewish king in Jerusalem. Jesus told them, "You don't get it."

In the shortest and most sweeping Bible study ever conducted, Jesus explained the entire Bible to them: "And beginning with Moses and all the Prophets, he explained to them what was said in all the Scriptures concerning himself" (Luke 24:27).

Ironically (and tragically) the people who opposed Jesus most strenuously were the religious leaders. They knew the Bible inside and out, but they missed Jesus.

Ironically (and tragically) the people who opposed Jesus most strenuously were the religious leaders. They knew the Bible inside and out, but they missed Jesus. They were so focused on doing things *for* God that they couldn't receive the gift of grace *from* God (John 5:39–40).

The Bible is a mirror revealing the plan of God, the greatness and grace of God, and our new identity as His children. The more clearly we see Jesus in the pages of the Bible, the more we'll be amazed with Him—and the more we're amazed with Him, the more we'll be blown away with His magnificent love and our astounding new identity in Him. The demands, compulsion, and condemnation that defined us before no longer have the power to define us now.

What does the Bible actually say about our new identity in Christ? We could look at many things, but we'll focus on two: adoption and a perfect record.

Children of God. A young couple recently adopted a baby girl. In the state of Texas, the legal process is completed after six months when all legal rights of the birth parents are terminated and the baby is legally declared to be a member of the new family. When the judge issues the final decree and the adoption is finalized, nothing changes and everything changes. The baby doesn't look any different, and her diapers may not have magically been changed, but the status of the child has been radically and permanently transformed!

In Paul's second letter to the Corinthians, he went to great lengths to describe the wonder of salvation and the hope of resurrected bodies, "an eternal house in heaven." From the moment we trust in Christ as our Savior, we have a new identity as God's adopted children, a new relationship with Him, and a new destiny. That's why Paul could exclaim, "Therefore, if anyone is in Christ, the new creation has come: The old has gone, the new is here" (2 Cor. 5:17)!

Adopted children, especially if they're older than newborns, often take time to adjust to their new parents. They may have been shuttled between orphanages and foster homes, and they wondered if they would ever find anyone to love them and be committed to them. Fear, then, is normal, but the certainty of the new relationship assures the adopted children of the new parents' affection. In the same way, the gospel tells us that our legal status has forever changed, and God, the perfect parent, assures His children of His undying affection and attention. Paul explained this point to the Roman Christians, not only assuring them of their new relationship with God, but also of their rightful inheritance as His children in His family:

> The Spirit you received does not make you slaves, so that you live in fear again; rather, the Spirit you received brought about your adoption to sonship. And by him we cry, 'Abba, Father.' The Spirit himself testifies with our spirit that we are God's children. Now if we are

children, then we are heirs—heirs of God and co-heirs with Christ, if indeed we share in his sufferings in order that we may also share in his glory. (Rom. 8:15–17)

Amazingly, this means God loves us with the same intensity, warmth, and devotion with which He loves Jesus (John 17:23). In his book, *Knowing God*, author and professor J. I. Packer explains that adoption means we're as accepted by the Father as Jesus:

> God . . . loves us with the same steadfast affection with which He eternally loves His beloved only-begotten. There are no distinctions of affection in the divine family. We are all loved just as fully as Jesus is loved. It is like a fairy story—the reigning monarch adopts waifs and strays to make princes of them—but praise God, it is not a fairy story: it is hard and solid fact, founded on the bedrock of free and sovereign grace. This, and nothing less than this, is what adoption means. No wonder that John cries, "Behold, what manner of love . . . !" When once you understand adoption, your heart will cry the same.[7]

Paul seems to make a special point of explaining our adoption in his letters. In the opening section of his letter to the Ephesians, he uses glowing language to describe our new identity as God's children. He makes the points that God has chosen us, adopted us, forgiven us, and sealed us in the relationship by the Holy Spirit. All of these blessings aren't doled out grudgingly by a stingy God. No, they are poured out "to the praise of his glorious grace, which he has freely given us in the One he loves . . . in accordance with the riches of God's grace that he lavishes on us" (Eph. 1:6–7).

Do you delight to give extravagant gifts to those you love? So does God.

A Perfect Record. Those of us with sensitive hearts, guilty consciences, or even a glimpse of the darkness in our hearts will protest, "Wait a minute! I'm not worthy! God can't possibly love and accept me after all I've done . . . and because of who I am!"

If our acceptance and security in Christ were based on our performance, all of us would be sunk! Even the most noble and obedient among us fall infinitely short of God's perfect, blinding holiness. But we don't stand before God holding *our* record. Jesus has given us *His* record of righteousness, goodness, faithfulness, and loyalty to the Father.

One of the most important but often overlooked characters in the gospels is Barabbas, a rebel who had committed murder. He had been caught and imprisoned, destined for execution on a Roman cross. When Jesus was brought before Pilate, the governor offered to release one prisoner during the Passover as a gesture of good faith. Pilate wanted to release Jesus, but the crowd shouted, "No, not him! Give us Barabbas" (John 18:40)! The rebel was set free and the innocent Son of God was led to the cross. That is the essence of biblical Christianity: Jesus looks at each one of us who is guilty and deserves to die, and He says, "I'll die in that person's place. I'll take the punishment they deserve, and I'll give them the righteous record I deserve."

To make the point even more poignant, look at the rebel's name: *Bar* means "son of," and *abbas* means "father." Barabbas, then, means "son of the father." Jesus took Barabbas' place, and Barabbas is emblematic of us all. Jesus, the true Son of the Father, died in our place so that we can also become sons of the Father.

This is, undoubtedly, the most astounding swap in all of history. Paul explained it this way: "God made him who had no sin to be sin for us, so that in him we might become the righteousness of God" (2 Cor. 5:21). We were "in Him" in Christ's death, and we are "in Him" in His life. And amazingly, now He lives His life in us.

How bad are our sins, including self-righteousness? They required the death of God's Son to pay for them. How valuable are we to God? He loves us so much He was willing to pay the ultimate price to have us as His own, and He credits all the goodness, moral perfection, and love of Jesus to our account. That's the extent of God's love for us.

Relocating Our Identity

Grace, and all it implies in our new relationship with God as His children who stand before Him with Jesus' record, is a free gift. As this revelation seeps deep into our hearts, we're melted and molded to become more like Him. The problem, though, is that we are so used to our old identity that the new one seems odd to us. We've gotten our sense of value and security (or at least, we've tried to get them) from two primary sources: our accomplishments and our ability to please others. We've believed achievement and approval would give us the joy, the meaning, and the security we've longed for—and for a while, they did. When the feeling didn't last, we tried even harder or gave up entirely.

The desire for love, approval, pleasure, and control isn't necessarily wrong. Augustine noticed that we have "disordered loves," in other words, we love lesser things supremely and the supreme things too little. The answer isn't to stop loving, but to reorder our loves so that we love God with all our hearts, then our neighbors as ourselves, and somewhere down the list, we enjoy approval and accomplishments as gifts from God. But remember, we love Him only because He loved us first. Our love for Him is always and only a response to His affection for us.

Too often, Christians believe they need to suppress their desires, but this effort only leads to frustration and guilt. There has to be another way. Many years ago, the famous Scottish pastor Thomas Chalmers preached a sermon titled "The Expulsive Power of a New Affection." He noted that no person, power, or possession ultimately satisfies our deepest longing. Instead of focusing our attention on the negative ("Just stop loving the wrong things"), he suggested that we set our hearts on "another object, even God, as more worthy of its attachment, so as that the heart shall be prevailed upon not to resign an old affection, which shall have nothing to succeed it, but to exchange an old affection for a new one."[8]

The radically new affection must be overwhelmingly powerful, beautiful, attractive, and compelling to capture our hearts so that all other desires are expelled from the center of our affections. There is only one thing that lovely, that wonderful, and that life changing: Jesus Christ.

When our hearts drift back to performance, pride, and fear, we need to contemplate, consider, and meditate on the wonders of God's greatness and grace.

To expel the old affections and replace them with Jesus, we have to do the hard work of thinking. When our hearts drift back to performance, pride, and fear, we need to contemplate, consider, and meditate on the wonders of God's greatness and grace. Some might complain, "That's hard!" Yes, it takes some time and discipline to reorient our hearts to the wonder of grace, but that's a lot easier and more productive than living on the endless treadmill of trying to do enough to win acclaim and approval! Actually, it's easier to renew your mind to embrace and experience God's gift of grace than to constantly struggle to grasp something that's always out of reach.

The treasure of God's grace is already ours. God isn't stingy. He has lavished it on us! In is brief letter to Philemon, Paul told him how he was praying for him: "I pray that your partnership with us in the faith may be effective in deepening your understanding of every good thing we share for the sake of Christ" (Philem. 6). You and I already have "every good thing" from God, but we need to be reminded again and again. When we know what we already have in Christ, faith goes to work!

We don't pursue this new affection alone. We need others to remind us, and they need us to remind them, of the glory of grace. From what I read in Paul's letters, he spent a lot of ink pointing people to grace as the source of their comfort, hope, and power. That's a good model for me as a husband, a father, a friend, and a leader. My main task is no longer controlling people so they'll do what I want them to do to make me look better. It's to point them to Jesus and encourage them to love Him with all their hearts. If they do that, motivation, obedience, joy, and love will surely follow.

But forgetting is easy. Isaiah told the people of God: "You have forgotten God your Savior; you have not remembered the Rock, your fortress" (Isa. 17:10). Isaiah, Paul, and all the other writers of the Scriptures never stop reminding us of our need to become sponges soaking up the grace of God.

Many of us in the church have the wrong view of accountability. For a long time, we got together with people to point out their failures and sins, and we told them, "You'd better do better than that! Come on!" Guilt has worked on a lot of people for a long time, but it only produces fear, not glad obedience.

In my family and in our church, I'm trying to create a very different culture of responsibility and accountability. When a group of people lives according to grace and reinforces our new identity in Christ, we spend our time reminding each other of the goodness of God and His incredible love for us. If someone fails, we assure that person of forgiveness and trust the Spirit of God to bring growth and healing. No condemnation, no manipulation. We go back again and again to the bedrock truth of God's grace, our adoption, and the righteousness credited to us in Christ. It is my hope and prayer that when people get up and leave these meetings, they don't feel belittled; they feel loved and inspired!

Paul's Heart, My Heart

Let me be painfully honest: for years, I was more concerned *that* people obeyed God's commands than *why* they obeyed. When they didn't jump through the hoops I described for them, and even when they were slow to jump, I felt like a failure . . . which made me more intent on getting them to obey—for the wrong reasons! Oh, I had plenty of ammunition to use on people. As I looked out over the audience, I saw people who had drifted from obedience, and I saw people who could care less about God. Some of them were coming to church just to please their spouse or kids or parents. I believed it was my duty to set them straight.

Somewhere on my journey toward grace, I read Paul's letter to the Corinthians. If I thought I had disobedient people in church, the church in Corinth had far more . . . and far more varieties! But Paul, the grace-filled pastor, pleaded with them instead of barking orders. At one point in his first letter, he stopped to explain his heart, his motivation, and his desire for them:

> I'm not writing all this as a neighborhood scold just to make you feel rotten. I'm writing as a father to you, my children. I love you and want you to grow up well, not spoiled. There are a lot of people around who can't wait to tell you what you've done wrong, but there aren't many fathers willing to take the time and effort to help you grow up. It was as Jesus helped me proclaim God's Message to you that I became your father. I'm not, you know, asking you to do anything I'm not already doing myself. . . . So how should I prepare to come to you? As a severe disciplinarian who makes you toe the mark? Or as a good friend and counselor who wants to share heart-to-heart with you? You decide. (1 Cor. 4:14–16, 21, MSG)

God began to change the way I look at people, what I want for them, and how to motivate them. I no longer preach to make people feel guilty enough to jump through hoops. I speak to them as a loving father talks to his children. Like a strong, tender dad, I sometimes have to say hard things to help people grow up, but I say those things to protect them, not to control them, and to bless them, not to intimidate them. I want people to bask in the warmth and power of God's love so they do the right things for the right reasons. I don't stand in the pulpit to make people behave; I stand there as their friend, their fellow traveler, and their counselor who wants to touch their hearts with the wonder of God's love, forgiveness, grace, and strength.

Known and Loved

All of us long to be fully known and fully loved—at the same time. If we think someone knows our deepest secrets but doesn't love us, we're terrified. If someone expresses love for us but doesn't really know us, it feels odd and awkward. Being fully known makes us vulnerable, and being fully loved gives us complete security. That's how God relates to us.

At a women's conference, Kim spoke on Psalm 139. She explained that King David beautifully described God's intimate and encyclopedic knowledge of us. He knows where we are and what we're thinking, even before we speak a word. David's confidence in God's love led him to a sense of awe, "This is too much, too wonderful—I can't take it all in" (Ps. 139:6, MSG)! He realizes he can travel east and west, but God is always with him. He can go up to heaven or down to hell, but God is there with him, too. Even darkness doesn't hide him from God because God can see even in the blackest darkness—of the night or of our hearts. David reflects on the marvel of God's creation, and he concludes, "I thank you, High God— you're breathtaking! Body and soul, I am marvelously made! I worship in adoration—what a creation" (Ps. 139:15, MSG)!

David was thoroughly convinced he had no secrets from God, and he could never escape God's loving presence. He was perfectly known and deeply loved. The reality of his vulnerability and security captured the king's heart. Instead of being bored with spiritual things or rebelling against God out of fear, David's heart melted in wonder and affection. He told God,

> Your thoughts—how rare, how beautiful!
> God, I'll never comprehend them!
> I couldn't even begin to count them—
> any more than I could count the sand of the sea.
> Oh, let me rise in the morning and live always with you!
> (Ps. 139:17–19, MSG)

Are God's thoughts rare and beautiful to you? When a music lover hears her favorite song, she lingers over every note and word. It's delightful. When an art lover stands in front of a famous painting, he notices every brushstroke from the master's hand. When a naturalist studies an endangered animal, she is absorbed in the details of the animal's life. My point is this: when we find God beautiful and delightful, we don't have to force ourselves to think about Him. We can't stop thinking about Him! We're like lovers who can't get enough of each other. That's because God created us—and recreated us—to be His bride, His lover, His cherished treasure.

Because of grace, we don't have to hide anymore. Because of grace, we don't have to lie anymore. Because of grace, we don't have to blame others for our faults, or minimize them, or deny they even happened. Because of grace, we're totally known and fully loved. We can be vulnerable because there's no risk of ridicule or rejection from God.

In his beautiful treatise on the Christian life in the middle of his letter to the Romans, Paul begins by assuring us, "Therefore, there is now no condemnation for those who are in Christ Jesus," and he ends with the promise, "For I am convinced that neither death nor life, neither angels nor demons, neither the present nor the future, nor any powers, neither height nor depth, nor anything else in all creation, will be able to separate us from the love of God that is in Christ Jesus our Lord" (Rom. 8:1, 38–39).

In between "no condemnation" and "no separation," Paul reminds us that the Holy Spirit is at work to whisper assurance, transform our hearts, and remind us that the promise of bodily resurrection is sure and true. In all of this, we find again and again that Christ is our greatest treasure . . . and we are His.

Grace is God as heart surgeon, cracking open your chest, removing your heart—poisoned as it is with pride and pain—and replacing it with his own.

—Max Lucado

Consider this . . .

1. In what ways is Christ our true and greatest treasure? How is this perception of Him different than seeing Him as a "specially attentive waiter"?

2. How would it change your self-concept—your purpose, your motivation, and your desires—if you really believed you were God's treasure?

3. How are the thirst for accomplishment and approval poor substitutes for the experience of God's love and acceptance?

4. If a friend asked you to explain "the expulsive power of a new affection," what would you say?

5. Why is it so hard to "relocate our identity"? What does it take to think deeply enough and challenge wrong perceptions so that our new identity in Christ becomes more real to us?

6. What is God saying to you in this chapter?

5 REST AND WRESTLING

> I do not at all understand the mystery of grace—
> only that it meets us where we are but does not
> leave us where it found us.
>
> **—Anne Lamott**

Before I began to grasp the wonder of grace, I tried my best to earn approval, to win respect, and to impress people. I was driven to be the best leader I could be, but not out of compassion for those I was leading. It was all about proving myself. I was constantly checking myself out by looking in the mirror of others' success. I read their posts on Twitter and Facebook. I noticed how many followers they had and how many visits they had to their blogs. I searched to find out what people were saying about me—and I lived or died by the words I saw on my phone or computer screen.

When things went wrong, I had to find someone to blame. I tore myself apart with vicious condemnation. I guess I thought self-hatred would produce good results. I told myself over and over again that I wasn't a good enough husband, father, friend, or leader, but I didn't reserve my wrath for myself. Kim, the kids, our staff, and anyone who breathed could be the target of my fierce judgment.

Real Rest

Sometimes, people noticed how driven and burned out I'd become, and they would say, "Ben, you need to take a break. Take a few days to rest."

Rest? I didn't know how. I sometimes stopped my frantic activity for a few hours or a few days, but my mind couldn't stop churning. I had to figure out a way to do more, be more, and accomplish more. My body might be in neutral, but my thoughts were always in overdrive.

Oh, I prayed during all those years, but my prayers were that God would make me more effective. I wanted God to help me be more driven, more demanding, and more successful. God's power was the means to my success, and His love was a pipedream.

The endless and grueling treadmill of performance isn't just a problem for pastors. It's a tendency for every believer because we naturally prefer to prove ourselves instead of humbly accepting the gift of God's grace. Our frantic and compulsive efforts make us blind and foolish. They make us think we can do enough to achieve ultimate fulfillment through our hard work, intelligence, and skills, and we focus all our attention on the gifts rather than the giver. We try to convince ourselves we're doing all our work for God, but we're really using Him to make us more successful instead of adoring and honoring Him. We've forgotten our greatest joy, and we've settled for a life of false promises, brief blips of feeling good, and long seasons of fear, self-condemnation, and shame.

Finally, when the kindness of God led me to repentance, His grace obliterated the treadmill! I don't know why I'd missed it for so long, but when Jesus' love captured my heart, a radical transformation happened in the deepest part of my soul. Suddenly, a new world of affection, joy, freedom, and meaning opened before my eyes—and it was all about Jesus. On the treadmill, I'd lived in a narrow tunnel with my eyes focused on the next step I had to take, the next goal I had to meet, and the next person I had to impress. I lived in constant fear that I wouldn't measure up, yet with arrogance that I could make life work. The grace of God—His unmerited, undeserved, crazy affection for me—shattered all those misguided assumptions about God, about life, and about myself. No dramatic building implosion we sometimes see on the local news could have been more necessary and welcome. My old presumptions had to be blasted into dust.

I had been desperately looking for acceptance, and then I realized the only One whose opinion really matters completely, warmly embraced me. I had tried to impress people so they would validate me, but then I understood that being "in Christ" brought more validation than any achievement in the world. I had pursued security by striving for success, but I finally grasped that true security, the kind that could never be taken away, was already mine because Jesus had paid the ultimate price for me and the Father had adopted me as His own. I had been on a treasure hunt to find the meaning of life, but I had failed to realize that I already owned the greatest treasure the world has ever known. I already had Jesus.

I stopped striving and started resting in the loving arms of God. We sometimes talk about peace as if it's a disconnected sensation. It's actually what happens when we stop trying and start trusting, when we stop pushing and start relaxing in the goodness and greatness of God. Peace comes when we believe the gospel. Jesus invites us,

"Are you tired? Worn out? Burned out on religion? Come to me. Get away with me and you'll recover your life. I'll show you how to take a real rest. Walk with me and work with me—watch how I do it. Learn the unforced rhythms of grace. I won't lay anything heavy or ill-fitting on you. Keep company with me and you'll learn to live freely and lightly." (Matt. 11:28–30, MSG)

"Unforced rhythms of grace" is the song of God's love for each of us. The problem is that many of us are trying to dance, but we can't hear the music God is playing. I didn't hear it for a long time, but I'm dancing now!

Walking with God became fun; it became an adventure when I stopped trying to earn God's acceptance and embraced the magnificent truth that by faith I was already in Jesus, the recipient of all His love, all His strength, and all His wisdom. I could finally relax.

True spiritual rest comes from a radical reorientation of our concept of God so that we see His smile instead of imagining His frown. Rest doesn't come from striving, but from trusting the One who demonstrated His love by paying the ultimate price for us. Rest simply refers to an inner posture of trust and strong confidence in Jesus' finished work and His gracious purposes for us.

Effortless?

For years, I heard some pastors and read some authors who said the Christian life is "effortless." That seemed utterly ludicrous to me. My life was a continual grind, with the agonizing torment of knowing I never measured up but not having any way to stop trying. I was always wrestling—with God to bless me, with myself because I knew I wasn't good enough, and with everyone else because I was afraid their failure would tarnish my reputation. And I couldn't stand that!

I had been searching frantically for God's
blessings, favor, love, and acceptance, but
they were already mine. I just didn't realize it.

Grace changed everything. I had been searching frantically for God's blessings, favor, love, and acceptance, but they
were already mine. I just didn't realize it. The promises of the
abundant life were already fulfilled, but I had been living like
a beggar. I had always assumed God was angry with me, that
I could never do enough to please Him, but I knew I needed
to keep trying as long as I was alive. The revelation of grace
gave me a categorically new and different picture of God: He
is smiling at me! He's in a good mood, and He wants to spend
time with me.

What face did people see when Jesus walked the earth?
Certainly, He spoke with defiance when He defended the grace
of God to the obstinate Pharisees, but if we read the Gospels
carefully, a different face may emerge. A friend of mine was
on a trip to India, and he helped set up a showing of the film
Jesus in a village outside Bangalore. Some of his group set up
the projector and strung up a sheet between two trees. As the
sun went down, he and some others went from house to house
(actually, hut to hut) to invite people to come to the center
of the village to watch the film. He had seen the movie many
times, but he had never heard it in Hindi. This time, he watched
the scenes even more closely. In the middle of the film, he was
struck by a fact he had missed before: Jesus was smiling! In
scene after scene, Jesus warmly greeted people, touched them
tenderly, and spent time with them—not because He had to,
but because He genuinely loved them. My friend told me, "I had

read about the love of Jesus since I was a kid, and I had heard countless messages about it, but until that night, I didn't really believe it. I went back and read the Gospels again, and I saw the tender, patient love of Jesus on almost every page!"

Jesus wasn't just kind and loving with "good people." A Pharisee invited Jesus and His followers to have dinner with him, but when they came, the host didn't extend to Jesus the most basic courtesies of washing His feet and welcoming Him with a kiss. At the formal dinner, a woman barged in—uninvited and unwanted by the host. We can assume that Jesus had met her earlier, and she had been amazed by His love. In response, she "came there with an alabaster jar of perfume. As she stood behind him at his feet weeping, she began to wet his feet with her tears. Then she wiped them with her hair, kissed them and poured perfume on them" (Luke 7:37–38).

The Pharisee was indignant, but Jesus didn't take the side of the religious leader against an outcast. He pointed to the woman as an example of a sinner who has been touched by grace. Jesus is thrilled when anyone—especially a person who seems hopelessly lost—turns to Him and accepts His offer of love and acceptance.

We can also see Jesus' tender love in His response to personal betrayal. Peter was the chief spokesman of the disciples. At dinner on the night of the arrest, Jesus again predicted His death, now only hours away. Peter boldly assured Jesus, "I will lay down my life for you" (John 13:37). Jesus knew better. He told Peter that before the night was over, Peter would betray Him—not once, not twice, but three times before a cock crowed.

As Jesus led His men to the garden late that night, He asked three of them, Peter, James, and John, to pray with him. In the hour when He needed their support and comfort as He faced an excruciating death, they fell asleep. A few minutes later, a band of soldiers came to arrest Him. They took Him to be tried by Annas, the acting high priest. As Jesus was being questioned, Peter stood outside warming himself near a charcoal fire. Three people asked if he was a follower of Jesus, and each time, he denied even knowing Jesus. After the last denial, a cock crowed. Peter's eyes met the eyes of Jesus, and the shattered and humiliated disciple wept bitter tears of shame.

After the resurrection, Peter wasn't sure where he stood with Jesus. At one point, it appears that Peter gave up on the whole enterprise of discipleship and went back to his old profession of fishing. One morning after catching nothing all night, Peter and his friends saw a man on the beach. The man told them to cast their nets again, and they miraculously brought in an enormous haul of large fish! Peter knew it was Jesus. He threw himself into the water and swam to shore as quickly as possible. When he got there, Jesus was waiting. He had cooked some fish and bread for the men's breakfast over a charcoal fire.

Three times, Jesus asked Peter, "Do you love me?" And three times, Peter answered, "Yes, You know I love You." Jesus went to great lengths to assure his friend of the magnitude of His love and forgiveness. Peter had given up on Jesus, but Jesus hadn't given up on him. Peter had denied Jesus three times; now he had the opportunity to express his affection and loyalty three times. The charcoal fire that morning reminded Peter of his greatest sin. Jesus didn't want His friend to miss the point: Jesus hadn't excused his betrayal, and He hadn't reduced it to something less offensive. The aroma of the charcoal reminded Peter of the depths of his failure . . . so he could enjoy the full depths of Jesus' love, forgiveness, and acceptance (John 21:1–19).

Some of us, like the prostitute who came in uninvited to pour out her love for Jesus, have committed many "younger brother" sins. Jesus gladly welcomes us, forgives us, and cherishes us. Others are prideful and self-reliant, like Peter and the "elder brother" in Jesus' story of the prodigal. Jesus goes out of His way to show us the full extent of our self-righteousness (which we thought was a virtue), and assures us that He fully forgives. When He relates to both kinds of people, Jesus smiles. When people ignore or refuse to respond to Him in faith, hope, and love, He isn't indignant, and He doesn't smirk with sarcasm. When the rich young man insisted on trusting in his obedience as a means of earning credit with God, Jesus "looked at him and loved him" (Mark 10:21).

Our concept of God directly affects our outlook on life and our relationships. My concept of God had been angry and demanding, so I became angry and demanding of myself and everyone around me. In *Grace: The Power to Change*, Dr. James Richards observes that we want to grow in our faith and experience the fruit of the Spirit, but our growth is shaped by our view of God:

> One of the greatest hindrances to bringing about positive change is the way we see God, the way we see Jesus. Try as you may, if you have a negative view of God, you cannot become a positive Christian. If you see God as angry, you will be angry. If you see God as vengeful, you will be full of vengeance. If you see God as fault-finding, you will be fault-finding. You are continually being changed into the image of the God you believe in. That change happens without effort on your part. It is happening by the power of believing.[9]

In describing the Christian life, I think the word *effortless* is a bit overstated, but it makes a point. Before grace began changing me, my life was anything but effortless. I saw myself as a slave. I worked like crazy, but always to please an angry master. When I finally saw that this master was actually my loving Father, my motivation and my source of power both radically changed.

Suddenly, I wanted to please the One who loved me so much, and I tapped into the limitless power of God, the same power that raised Jesus from the tomb! Jesus has become my life. Jesus has become my meaning. Jesus has become my strength. Jesus has become my delight.

When a man loves to play golf, does he consider it a burden to clean his clubs, call his friends to plan the date, and practice so he can do well? No! All of these things are part of the joy of playing the game. When two lovers want to know each other, do they despise the fact that they have to give up doing other things so they can be together? No, they can't wait to stare into each other's eyes. When a man wants to take his little league son to a major league game, does he worry about spending money for the tickets? No, he can't wait to share his love of the game. In the same way, when we delight in Jesus and we're convinced He delights in us, life is no longer a grind, serving God is no longer a pain, reading the Bible is no longer an imposition, and giving is no longer something we resent. We *want* to be with God, we *want* to know Him better, we *want* others to know Him, and we *want* to please Him in every way we can. Paul told the Corinthians that the love of God, fully and finally demonstrated in the sacrifice of Jesus on the cross, had radically changed him from the inside out:

> Christ's love has moved me to such extremes. His love has the first and last word in everything we do. Our firm decision is to work from this focused center: One man died for everyone. That puts everyone in the same boat. He included everyone in his death so that everyone could also be included in his life, a resurrection life, a far better life than people ever lived on their own. (2 Cor. 5:13–15, MSG)

Some people have objected, "Yes, but what about God's judgment? What about the law and God's requirements of obedience? You can't leave that out!" Indeed. The Bible is very clear that all of us are sinners under the penalty of death. The law accuses us, and it's right. How does God make us right with Him when the law condemns us? Paul told them, "Look at the cross. Your answers are found there."

God presented Christ as a sacrifice of atonement, through the shedding of his blood—to be received by faith. He did this to demonstrate his righteousness, because in his forbearance he had left the sins committed beforehand unpunished—he did it to demonstrate his righteousness at the present time, so as to be just and the one who justifies those who have faith in Jesus. (Rom. 3:25–26)

When Jesus died on the cross, do we find God's law? Yes, the fact that the law condemns us as unholy and unrighteous requires a drastic payment, the payment of death. Do we find God's love when we look to the cross? Yes! Christ loves us so much that He was willing to die the death we deserved to die. So in the law, God was *just* in condemning sin on the cross, and in grace, He was "*the one who justifies* those who have faith in Jesus."

This wasn't a theological construction a bright young Jew came up with decades after Jesus lived, died, and was raised again. Over and over again, Jesus predicted that He would be betrayed and killed (Mark 8:31–33; 9:30–32; 10:32–34). Not long before He was arrested, the Father's voice boomed out of heaven to validate the Son. Some people thought it was thunder, and others assumed an angel had spoken to Him.

Jesus said, "This voice was for your benefit, not mine. Now is the time for judgment on this world; now the prince of this world will be driven out. And I, when I am lifted up from the earth, will draw all people to myself." He said this to show the kind of death he was going to die. (John 12:30–33, MSG)

Jesus said God's judgment was certain, but He had a solution. He would draw all kinds of people—Jews and Gentiles—to Himself only by drawing all judgment to Himself. All the wrath—the righteous wrath of a holy God—was poured out on Him so it wouldn't have to be poured out on us. That's the measure of His love.

The cross points to Jesus as the only hope of getting off the treadmill of performance, guilt, and pride.

The cross points to Jesus as the only hope of getting off the treadmill of performance, guilt, and pride. The death of Jesus is the clearest, boldest statement that the law is God's standard, but none of us can hope to fulfill it. We were helpless and hopeless, but God sent a Savior. Now, we don't obey to earn God's favor, we obey because we already have God's favor. We don't give and serve to earn points with God so we can twist His arm and convince Him we deserve His blessings. We are already the richest, most blessed beings in the universe, so we give and serve because we want to resemble the family likeness.

When the meaning of the gospel sinks deep into us, it makes a difference in every thought, motive, word, and action.

We become a little more like God—extravagant in our love, tender, compassionate, wise, and welcoming. We're no longer afraid of the truth; we live in truth. We're no longer afraid to admit we're wrong; we know we're often wrong, but God loves us still. We're no longer afraid to reach out to people who are very different from us; Jesus, the infinitely holy God, reached out to people who were very, very different from Him: you and me.

With grace, we no longer have to look over our shoulders constantly to see if anyone sees how important we are. We realize that God knows the worst about us, and He loves us anyway. We are deeply flawed but even more deeply loved.

The grace of God provides ultimate security, so there's no need for frantic action. The grace of God provides the assurance of His love, so there's no fear of rejection. The grace of God provides something I desperately wanted but had no idea how to find—real rest.

Clarity about the Cross

Many Christians are confused about the central truth of our faith. The cross of Christ provides clarity—about the nature of Jesus, His grace, and all the promises of our new life in Him— but many of us have a limited understanding of what the cross accomplished for us. We can understand it by asking three questions: (1) What did we lose at the cross? (2) What did we gain at the cross? (3) And what did we retain at the cross? Let's examine these questions.[10]

(1) What did we *lose* at the cross? When we trust in Jesus' sacrificial death, He identifies with us, and we identify with Him. He died *for* us, and we died *in* Him. To put it another way, we were in Christ when He died, so we died with Him. Paul explained, "Could it be any clearer? Our old way of life was nailed to the cross with Christ, a decisive end to that sin-miserable life—no longer at sin's every beck and call" (Rom. 6:6, MSG)! The only way we could escape slavery to the obligations and punishment of the law was to die. We couldn't fulfill it, and we couldn't impress God by our innate goodness. We had no hope at all. Our only way out was to die. Our "old nature," "old man," and "old way of life" were beyond reforming. When Jesus died, we died in Him and with Him.

This means that the full weight of guilt and shame our old nature deserved is dead, too. All our sins have been forgiven (Ps. 103:12; Rom. 8:1)—past, present, and future. Remember, all of our sins were future when Jesus paid the price for them.

Ironically, before we trusted Jesus, we thought we were alive, but we were spiritually dead. Our old nature is fueled by pride and fear, is driven to perform, and hides or excuses flaws. Paul compares our previous condition to a debtor's prison. In the Roman world, people who couldn't pay their debts were thrown into jail, and a list of their debts was nailed to the cell door. Paul paints the picture for us:

> When you were dead in your sins and in the uncircumcision of your flesh, God made you alive with Christ. He forgave us all our sins, having canceled the charge of our legal indebtedness, which stood against us and condemned us; he has taken it away, nailing it to the cross. And having disarmed the powers and authorities, he made a public spectacle of them, triumphing over them by the cross. (Col. 2:13–15)

Notice what happened. God didn't just open the cell door and let us go. Our debt had to be paid, so Jesus took our list of charges and nailed them to His cell door, the cross. There, it was "paid in full." The forces of darkness delighted to see us in prison, but Jesus triumphed over them, mocking them in a public display on Calvary of His power, humility, and affection.

At the cross we also lost our fear of the law. It had always pointed to our failings and sins . . . and it was right in its negative assessment! But the cross took the sting of the law away. Paul explained, "For when we were in the realm of the flesh, the sinful passions aroused by the law were at work in us, so that we bore fruit for death. But now, by dying to what once bound us, we have been released from the law so that we serve in the new way of the Spirit, and not in the old way of the written code" (Rom. 7:5–6).

We also lost something else important: our bondage to the comparison, pressure, and demands. To the Galatians, Paul wrote, "May I never boast except in the cross of our Lord Jesus Christ, through which the world has been crucified to me, and I to the world" (Gal. 6:14). To Paul and to us, the attraction of the world—riches, physical beauty, power, prestige, and control—no longer have any power over us. They don't just lose a little of their influence. Their power died when Jesus died for us. And the other side is also true: We are dead to the world. When the love of Jesus fills our hearts to the point of bursting, those things no longer entice us. Old sources of identity and security are replaced by something (someone) infinitely better and more beautiful. Performance anxiety begins to melt away. Fear of disapproval is dissolved by unending love. Comparison and pride cease to capture our hearts because our hearts are already captured.

We lost some extremely important things at the cross.

(2) What did we *gain* at the cross? The death of Jesus looked like the biggest tragedy the world had ever known; an innocent, loving man was cruelly murdered and seemingly forgotten. But God had an entirely different concept of the event.

At this singular moment in all of history, God opened His treasure chest and poured out immeasurable riches.

God gave us complete and utter forgiveness (Eph. 1:7, 2:8–9; Heb. 10:17, et al); total and warm acceptance (Eph. 1:6); the righteousness of Christ credited to us (Rom. 3:21–26); and tender, strong love (Eph. 2:4–5; Rom. 5:8).

We didn't just get information or good advice about how to live. God gave us the very life of Christ—He is our life (Col. 3:4). He has given us the Holy Spirit to assure us of His love, to pray for us when we can't pray (Rom. 8:26–27), and to empower us to live for God (Rom. 8:9–14). God imparted to us a radically new identity and a new status (Rom. 8:15–17; 2 Cor. 5:17).

We aren't alone. As we've seen, we have two Advocates: Jesus represents us to the Father when we sin (1 John 2:1), and the Holy Spirit argues for God's love, truth, and purposes to our hearts all day every day (Rom. 8:16).

When we rest in the grace of God, we become more passionate than ever—but for His glory instead of ours.

All of these treasures transform our "have tos" to "want tos," so sin no longer looks so attractive any more. We used to be driven by the lust for power, prestige, and possessions, but now we're led by the Spirit of God (Gal. 5:18). Ironically, when we rest in the grace of God, we become more passionate than ever—but for His glory instead of ours.

Good theology points us to a person. We've gained a Father in heaven who is supremely wise, powerful, and compassionate.

Our earthly fathers may have been wonderful, but they can't compare to this father! Or they may have abused us or abandoned us. Our heavenly Father delights in revealing how different He is from the one who hurt us.

When we ran from God, we may not have given Him a second thought. Many of us, however, gave Him plenty of thoughts—and most of them were filled with fear! Now we approach the presence of God with confidence (Heb. 4:16) because we know we're wanted. We might have seen ourselves as beggars who might get a few scraps from a harsh God, but now we know we're children of the King—"heirs of God and co-heirs with Christ" (Rom. 8:17).

We've also received a role in the family business of redeeming and restoring a lost world. We are Christ's ambassadors to a world that desperately needs to sense the love of God and hear the truth of the gospel of grace (2 Cor. 5:18–19). To fulfill our role, we have the presence, power, and purpose of the Spirit of God living inside us (1 Cor. 6:19–20).

At the cross, we gained something else that we desperately want: peace *with* God and the peace *of* God. We were enemies of God, but the cross turned us into His friends, children, and lovers. Because of Christ's full and final sacrifice to pay for our sins and to credit His righteousness to our account, we can "cease striving and know" that our God isn't angry with us any more. Paul wrote to the Romans, "Therefore, since we have been justified through faith, we have peace with God through our Lord Jesus Christ, through whom we have gained access by faith into this grace in which we now stand. And we boast in the hope of the glory of God" (Rom. 5:1–2).

The ground where we stand isn't shaky like it was when we depended on our efforts to prove and please. Grace is solid ground; Jesus is "the solid rock" where we can relax and stand secure. We have no fear of judgment because Jesus absorbed it all. We have no fear of being cast aside because the Father has adopted us. We have no fear of being alone because the Spirit whispers to us that we are God's dear children. That's the nature of "peace with God."

But that's not all. We also have the peace of God. Knowing God doesn't protect us from all harm. In fact, walking with God sometimes leads us into harm because we represent the King of glory to a defiant world. Hardships and heartaches come in many different ways: sickness, natural disasters, financial collapse, the sins of others, our own foolish choices, the attacks of the Enemy, old age, and death. Our natural tendency is to wonder, "Where's God? Doesn't He know? Doesn't He care?" Yes, He knows, He cares, and He's fully present with us in our pain. We can trust in the wisdom, sovereignty, goodness, and power of God, even when we can't see His hand at work or sense His presence. Paul endured all kinds of abuse and abandonment. When he talks about trusting God in difficult times, he's talking from experience! He encouraged the Philippian believers to trust God even in the most challenging situations:

> Rejoice in the Lord always. I will say it again: Rejoice! Let your gentleness be evident to all. The Lord is near. Do not be anxious about anything, but in every situation, by prayer and petition, with thanksgiving, present your requests to God. And the peace of God, which transcends all understanding, will guard your hearts and your minds in Christ Jesus. (Phil. 4:4–7)

Trusting the God of grace, then, gives us peace with God so that we aren't afraid of His righteous judgment any longer, and it gives us the peace of God as we face the anxieties and difficulties of our lives. Through it all, we can trust in the One who gave Himself for us.

(3) What did we *retain* at the cross? Some people read Paul's triumphant statement to the Corinthians, "The new creation has come: The old has gone, the new is here!" (2 Cor. 5:17), and they're confused. They hoped God would make their figures more attractive or their hair grow back in the bald spots, and they wanted Him to change their personalities. "The new" Paul was talking about is our status, our identity, our connection with God and His family, and our destiny. Some aspects of our lives, though, aren't new.

When we trust in the grace of God, our bodies don't change. Our "earthsuits" still get older, we still get sick, and we are still destined to die unless the Lord comes back before that day. Still, faith can be a significant benefit for our bodies. Studies by various health organizations show that anxiety, worry, and stress make people physically sick. According to the World Health Organization, about 70 percent of illnesses and 50 percent of deaths are the result of poor choices.[11] The American Psychological Association reports that more than half of Americans point to stress as a primary cause of health problems.[12] The peace of God replaces worry with trust and anxiety with peace. It can make a difference in our visits to the doctor!

Though our bodies don't suddenly change when we trust in Christ, the future of our bodies is radically altered. When Jesus was raised from the dead, He was the "firstfruit" (1 Cor. 15:20). We have the assurance that someday we will also be resurrected. Our bodies will be like the one Jesus had when He appeared to the disciples after He came out of the tomb. He was both spiritual and physical, He could walk through walls, but He could eat a fish and people could touch Him. Today, our bodies are breaking down, but someday, they'll be raised to permanent glory. Paul explained, "We know that the whole creation has been groaning as in the pains of childbirth right up to the present time. Not only so, but we ourselves, who have the firstfruits of the Spirit, groan inwardly as we wait eagerly for our adoption to sonship, the redemption of our bodies" (Rom. 8:22–23).

Our personalities didn't change when we trusted in Jesus. We didn't suddenly become bubbly and outgoing if we were quiet and reflective, and we didn't become instinctive risk-takers if we had been cautious. But our personalities were set free so we could fully become the people God created us to be. The old fears no longer limit us, and old compulsions no longer drive us to do dumb things. We are secure, loved, and free to follow God with all our hearts.

We retained another thing at the cross: our thinking patterns and perceptions didn't suddenly change. If we liked chocolate before we trusted Jesus, we'll probably still like chocolate. If we drove badly before, we probably still drive badly. But just as our personalities can be freed by the grace of God, our thoughts can be redirected. How? Just after Paul introduced the concept of the peace of God in his letter to the Philippians, he showed them that we experience the peace God has graciously given when we focus our minds on God's marvelous truth: "Finally, brothers and sisters, whatever is true, whatever is noble, whatever is right, whatever is pure, whatever is lovely, whatever is admirable—if anything is excellent or praiseworthy—think about such things. Whatever you have learned or received or heard from me, or seen in me—put it into practice. And the God of peace will be with you" (Phil. 4:8–9).

At the cross, we retain our bodies, our personalities and our thinking patterns, but all three will be radically changed sooner or later.

The Right Fight

Do grace-believing Christians still wrestle with spiritual things? Yes, of course, but not like before. Before grace captures us and convinces us that the death of Christ has fully justified us—forgiven us and credited us with His righteousness—we fought to earn God's love and acceptance, or more accurately, we fought to earn the respect of the people sitting next to us in the next pew or the next office. That's the wrong fight!

When we wrestle, strain, and struggle to prove ourselves to earn God's acceptance, we live by the law, and we die a thousand excruciating deaths by our repeated failures, and our pride is inflated when we think we're meeting standards. We're full of fear and pride, worry and shame. We're losing the battle even when we think we're doing well!

The church is full of "unbelieving believers." These people can recite the doctrines of Jesus dying on the cross, but in the depths of their hearts, they're convinced they still need to measure up to merit God's approval. They are insecure or cocky . . . or both. The wonder and beauty of God's abundant grace doesn't amaze them. I know how it feels. I was one of them far too long.

As we've seen, grace ends the most important fight of our lives. We acted like God's enemies, but now He is our dear Father. In his letter to the Colossians, Paul said that our new relationship with God gives us a new passport: We belong to a new King and a new kingdom. We give "joyful thanks to the Father, who has qualified you to share in the inheritance of his holy people in the kingdom of light. For he has rescued us from the dominion of darkness and brought us into the kingdom of the Son he loves, in whom we have redemption, the forgiveness of sins" (Col. 1:12–14). We are citizens of heaven (Phil. 3:20). The adoption papers have been signed. The transfer is complete. We belong to Him!

Our fight has changed, but it hasn't gone away. We no longer fight with God, but we have two other adversaries: the remnants of our sinful flesh (especially our unrenewed mind) and Satan, evil within and evil without. Paul described the fight with temptations and selfishness that still is part of our lives as grace-believing Christians:

> My counsel is this: Live freely, animated and motivated by God's Spirit. Then you won't feed the compulsions of selfishness. For there is a root of sinful self-interest in us that is at odds with a free spirit, just as the free spirit is incompatible with selfishness. These two ways of life are antithetical, so that you cannot live at times one way and at times another way according to how you feel on any given day. Why don't you choose to be led by the Spirit and so escape the erratic compulsions of a law-dominated existence? (Gal. 5:16–18, MSG)

Paul wasn't "talking down" to the Galatians. He experienced this internal conflict firsthand. In his letter to the Romans, after his beautiful and eloquent description of the power of the gospel and the fact that the power of the law no longer has any way to condemn us, he explained his own struggle:

> I do not understand what I do. For what I want to do I do not do, but what I hate I do. . . . As it is, it is no longer I myself who do it, but it is sin living in me. For I know that good itself does not dwell in me, that is, in my sinful nature. For I have the desire to do what is good, but I cannot carry it out. For I do not do the good I want to do, but the evil I do not want to do—this I keep on doing. (Rom. 7:15, 17–19)

Have you ever felt this way, even when you really wanted to please God? I have. I sometimes still do. What's the answer?

It's grace. Paul almost shouts, "What a wretched man I am! Who will rescue me from this body that is subject to death? Thanks be to God, who delivers me through Jesus Christ our Lord" (Rom. 7:24–25)! We can't fulfill the perfect law, but Jesus forgives us. We can't fulfill God's commands, but Jesus completely fulfilled them, and we're in Him. We're forgiven, we're loved, and we're secure. We don't just need the grace of God to enter the kingdom of God. We need to depend on the unmerited, limitless grace of God all day every day.

We need to get a fresh, profound, biblical grasp of our identity: We are saints, full-fledged members of God's family, but our behavior often falls short. We are saints who still sin, but the label is far more important and powerful. It's who we really are.

We're not schizophrenic, wondering who we are and where we belong. The truth of our new identity in Christ is fully established. The deal is done. However, we live between the "already" and the "not yet," between the sealing of the Holy Spirit to assure us of our relationship with Jesus (Eph. 1:13–14) and seeing Him face to face.

Our wrestling *with God* is over, but we still struggle *with the flesh's temptations and selfishness*. And there's another adversary that attacks us. We often look at the end of Paul's letter to the Ephesians to read about the "armor" we put on to do battle with the Enemy of our souls, but Paul actually refers to this struggle throughout his letter. In his prayer in the first chapter, he reminds us that the power of Christ is "far above all rule and authority, power and dominion, and every name that is invoked" (Eph. 1:21). These are orders of angelic and demonic beings. In the third chapter, he explains that the beauty and power of the gospel has been made known to those same "rulers and authorities in the heavenly realms" (Eph. 3:10). We fight against the plots and schemes of these forces by depending on the grace of God and all the resources He has given us to fight. In every situation, and against every adversary, we fight as children of the King of glory.

When I teach about the wonders of the grace of God, people sometimes come up to me with a puzzled expression on their faces and ask, "Uh, where did you get all that? I've read my Bible for years, but I haven't seen all this about grace." I'd like to blame "those preachers" who taught the Bible without pointing people to Jesus and His grace, but I first have to point the finger at me. For far too long, I taught the Bible as law, rules and demands, which produced only insecurity, compulsion, fear, and arrogance—certainly in me, and sadly in others. But thank God, that's changed! I've found true rest in the certainty of God's abundant, unconditional, persistent love. And now my fight isn't against Him any longer.

When grace happens, we receive not a nice compliment from God but a new heart. Give your heart to Christ, and he returns the favor.

—Max Lucado

Consider this . . .

1. How would you describe "the treadmill" of performance? What drives us to run so hard? What keeps us on it when it doesn't satisfy?

2. We become like the God we envision. Look at your life. What do your doubts, fears, ambitions, attitudes, relationships, and habits say about your view of God?

3. What does it mean that God is both "just and the justifier" of those who believe in Jesus? What is the significance of each?

4. How would you explain to a friend what we give up at the cross, what we gain, and what we retain? What concept in this section means the most to you? Explain your answer.

5. Why is it important to be certain that our status and our
    identity are totally secure, even though we still sin? How
    does this understanding give us rest and peace?

6. What is God saying to you in this chapter?

6 GRACE EVERY DAY

> **What gives me the most hope every day is God's grace; knowing that his grace is going to give me the strength for whatever I face, knowing that nothing is a surprise to God.**
>
> —**Rick Warren**

Many committed, sincere Christians long to experience the joy and freedom they find in the promises of God, but their future is blocked by their past. Thoughts of past wounds poison their minds with resentment and self-pity, and thoughts of past sins (especially those that are so big or so many) fill them with shame. Past relationships and events are further clouded by entrenched perceptions that God is angry. No matter what they do to impress Him and win His favor, it's never enough. For these people, every conversation, every goal, and every hope is haunted by the past.

Grace sets us free from the past, and it gives us a new way to think about the present and the future. When the revelation of God's limitless love swept over me, I realized I had a choice: I could shake my head at God's tender love and continue trying as hard as I could to make life work on my own, or I could take a deep breath, take God's hand, thank Him for His forgiveness, and look forward to the adventure of a new day walking with Him. I face that same choice every moment of every day.

A friend asked Kim what difference grace has made in my life. Her answer spoke volumes. She said, "Ben used to act cocky, like he knew it all, but it was all just a cover for his insecurity. Now he's less driven, more confident, and willing to admit when he's wrong because his sense of security is no longer in his ability to make people say, 'Wow!' when they see him. And he's not one person in public and another at home. He doesn't need to wear a mask any longer. He can be himself."

She's right. I don't live to impress people because the only One whose opinion really matters already knows the worst about me and loves me like crazy. The Lord spoke a message through Isaiah that perfectly describes how the righteousness credited to us in Christ transforms everything about us:

In righteousness you will be established:
Tyranny will be far from you;
you will have nothing to fear.
Terror will be far removed;
it will not come near you.
If anyone does attack you, it will not be my doing;
whoever attacks you will surrender to you.
(Isa. 54:14–15)

Today, I have been established in the righteousness of Jesus Christ. I am *in* Him, united *with* Him. The tyranny of trying to measure up has been removed from my life by the grace of God, and I have nothing to fear. The terror of condemnation, of the judgment of God and of people, won't come near me because Jesus' blood is my shield. If I slip back into the experience of tyranny and oppression, it's because I've forgotten the twin truths of justification: complete forgiveness and imputed righteousness. And God assures me that whenever I am attacked, it's not Him . . . it's *never* Him. When I go through difficulties, I don't have to wonder if God is punishing me. All of His righteous anger was spent on the perfect sacrifice, not on me.

Paul and Peter continually pointed to the gospel of grace as the source of spiritual vitality for all believers. In fact, we're not the only ones who should be continually amazed. Peter wrote that the Old Testament prophets looked forward to the Messiah who was to come to die and be raised to glory. "They clamored to know who and when. All they were told was that they were serving you, you who by orders from heaven have now heard for yourselves—through the Holy Spirit—the Message of those prophecies fulfilled. Do you realize how fortunate you are? Angels would have given anything to be in on this" (1 Peter 1:11–12, MSG)! We have a front-row seat to see and taste and experience the glory of God's amazing grace. The angels look from heaven and are stunned by what they see!

Are we bored by the gospel of grace? Do we think we're so advanced that we can be bothered and bored with grace? The angels don't think they're beyond it!

Think, Think, Think

All through the Bible, the writers encourage us to think, consider, contemplate, and meditate on God's truth to drive it deep into our minds and hearts. We have all kinds of firmly established perceptions in our minds, and most of them are wrong! We've looked at enough commercials, listened to enough friends, and heard enough songs to convince us that a headlong pursuit of power, prestige, and possessions will give us ultimate fulfillment. Those hopes don't die easily. We cling to them as long as we can.

We have an unrenewed mind that must be transformed by the gospel. Many Christians fill their minds with Scripture, but they focus on the law. After reading and studying the Bible, they feel more driven, more condemned, and more hopeless than ever. That's the effect of the law. It shows us how far short we fall from the perfection, wonder, and glory of God. For our minds to be renewed in the grace of God, we need to camp out with the gospel. In John's prologue, he described the difference between two sources: "For the law was given through Moses; grace and truth came through Jesus Christ" (John 1:17).

In the previous chapter, we saw that Paul told the Philippians to focus their thoughts on far better things, and his description perfectly fit the character of Christ: Who is true but Jesus? Who is more noble than Jesus? He is right, as pure as snow, more lovely than the most beautiful sunset, and the object of wonder, admiration, and praise. If we want to reframe our thinking, we need to think about the grace of Jesus, the tenderness and power of Jesus, the humility and glory of Jesus.

The radical reorientation of our thinking isn't optional. It's a matter of life and death.

The radical reorientation of our thinking isn't optional. It's a matter of life and death. In his letter to the Romans, Paul explained, "Those who live according to the flesh have their minds set on what the flesh desires; but those who live in accordance with the Spirit have their minds set on what the Spirit desires. The mind governed by the flesh is death, but the mind governed by the Spirit is life and peace" (Rom. 8:5–6).

Right thoughts about God, about His grace, about our identity, and about His purposes revolutionize the trajectory of our lives. A different lifestyle begins with what's going on between our ears, which then filters down into our hearts. In the same letter, Paul wrote, "Therefore, I urge you, brothers and sisters, in view of God's mercy, to offer your bodies as a living sacrifice, holy and pleasing to God—this is your true and proper worship. Do not conform to the pattern of this world, but be transformed by the renewing of your mind. Then you will be able to test and approve what God's will is—his good, pleasing and perfect will" (Rom. 12:1–2). Thinking—right thinking based on understanding the power of the gospel of grace—is essential if we want to experience God's presence, power, and purpose. But thinking rightly is one of the most challenging things we can do!

Our natural drift is away from the gospel toward self-effort . . . always with disastrous results. Martin Luther gave advice to pastors that every Christian should take as marching orders: "The gospel is the central article of the Christian faith. Most necessary is it that we learn it well, teach it to others, and beat it into their heads continually."[13] All of us can apply this principle to ourselves and ruthlessly root out legalism, moralism, and all forms of self-effort . . . and replace these poisons with the healing gospel of Christ.

Some people mistakenly believe that their radically new status as children of the King immediately protects them from fears and doubts. Then, when these painful feelings and negative thoughts arise, they're confused and discouraged. They wonder, *What's going wrong? Is grace not real? Did God leave me?* Actually, there's nothing wrong. They're just human, and they have more opportunities to think more deeply and clearly about the implications of the gospel in their goals, their relationships, and their hopes.

An old saying goes something like this: "We can't stop birds from flying over our heads, but we can keep them from building nests in our hair!" The point is that we can't keep thoughts from popping up in our minds, but we can do something about them. Instead of blaming ourselves for being such bad Christians, or giving up and letting our minds dwell on them endlessly, we can arrest them, consider their validity, throw out the destructive thoughts, and replace them with truth and grace. Peter instructed us,

> Therefore humble yourselves under the mighty hand of God, that He may exalt you in due time, casting all your care upon Him, for He cares for you. Be sober, be vigilant; because your adversary the devil walks about like a roaring lion, seeking whom he may devour. Resist him, steadfast in the faith, knowing that the same sufferings are experienced by your brotherhood in the world. (1 Peter 5:6–9, NKJV)

If we look carefully at the passage, Peter gives us an important insight about our spiritual conflict. Although Satan is our adversary who is sworn to destroy us, he's not the focus of a believer's struggle. For us, Satan is a defeated foe. Paul reminds us that Jesus completely conquered him and stripped him of all power and authority over us (Col. 2:15). As this translation points out, Satan doesn't devour who he *will*, but who he *may*. That's an important distinction. He can devour only those who aren't sober-minded and vigilant. Who are those people? This category includes anyone who forgets the gospel of grace— those who have drifted back to self-justification and believe their status with God depends on their efforts, goodness, and obedience. People who have drifted from the gospel are vulnerable to Satan's deceptions, temptations, and accusations.

Think of it this way: When a thief waits outside a bar, he's looking for a potential target who is too drunk to be aware of the danger and can't defend himself from the threat. Satan is like the thief; he's looking for people who are drunk on their own delusions of self-righteousness. We're vulnerable to his attacks only when we're too proud to admit we need grace. The humble, Peter implies, believe the truth, stay alert, and win the fight.

The real battle, then, is in our minds. When we humble ourselves and believe God's truth, grace flows into us and through us into the lives of those around us. Our minds become nimble and sharp. The Spirit of God makes us aware of the lies of the Enemy, the lies we believe from our past, the lies our friends tell us, and the lies of empty religion. If any message doesn't point us to the matchless grace of God and our new identity in Him, it's a lie!

Some people think they have to scream at the Devil to win the fight. That's not true. Jesus never yelled at Satan in the desert or at demons during His ministry. He simply spoke the truth. We don't shout Satan out, and we don't scream demons away. When we fill our minds and our voices with the truth of God, He gives us wisdom over the Enemy's schemes and power over his attacks.

But another factor threatens to knock us away from our position of strength: worry. Jesus told His followers: "Be careful, or your hearts will be weighed down with carousing, drunkenness and the anxieties of life, and that day will close on you suddenly like a trap. For it will come on all those who live on the face of the whole earth" (Luke 21:34–35). When our hearts are weighed down, we're preoccupied, we're not alert, and we're not vigilant. We're vulnerable to the Enemy's attacks. There's nothing wrong with being *concerned* about people or situations, but *worry* is the deep belief that we know better than

God how life ought to work. It's putting ourselves on the throne where only He belongs.

In spite of God's clear warnings and promises, Satan is devouring many of us because we still believe the lies of legalism and we're preoccupied by worries. Actually, the two are intricately related because they're both rooted in unbelief. Legalism and worry both lead to anxiety, fear, discouragement, drivenness, and depression. The condition is all too common, but God has given us a solution.

To have a sober mind, we have to fill it with scripts of grace and truth. We need to read the Bible and spend plenty of time in passages that proclaim the wonder of grace, our new identity, and the tenderness of God (like the dozens we've looked at in this book). We need to be around people who "get it," who are actively applying the gospel to every pursuit, every desire, and every relationship in their lives.

The old habits of thinking gradually melt in the warmth of God's grace, but some of our old thinking doesn't melt away—it has to be ruthlessly attacked! Paul used the imagery of siege warfare to illustrate the effort required to overcome errant hopes, flaming fears, misconceptions of God, and doubts about His love. He wrote the Corinthians: "For though we live in the world, we do not wage war as the world does. The weapons we fight with are not the weapons of the world. On the contrary, they have divine power to demolish strongholds. We demolish arguments and every pretension that sets itself up against the knowledge of God, and we take captive every thought to make it obedient to Christ" (2 Cor. 10:3–5).

The strongholds of fear and doubt may be strong, but God is far stronger.

In the fight, we're never on our own. The strongholds of fear and doubt may be strong, but God is far stronger. Our weapons are the gospel of grace and the power of the Spirit. A siege always takes time to wear down the opponent, but a surrounded, besieged city always falls sooner or later. We can be confident that we'll win, and new, rich, hopeful thoughts will fill our minds.

You Don't Have What It Takes

One of the most important points to learn if we're going to experience God's grace every day is to come to the humble realization that we don't have what it takes to make life work on our own. We've tried, and it hasn't worked out very well. We've been driven to achieve success, but we alienated the people we love and exhausted ourselves. We've tried to please people to win their approval, reading their minds so we could change our response to suit their every whim, but we lost ourselves in the process. We've been so hurt or so ashamed that we've withdrawn from any risk of being hurt again, but the sense of loneliness has almost killed us. If we're honest, we come to the conclusion that we simply don't have what it takes to live in joy, freedom, love, and strength. This perception is the beginning of humility.

Far too often, we've read the Bible in a way that only reinforces our compulsions to prove, please, and hide. For instance, one of the most common passages challenges us: "Whoever wants to be my disciple must deny themselves and take up their cross and follow me. For whoever wants to save their life will lose it, but whoever loses their life for me will find it" (Matt. 16:24–25). Our conclusion has been, "Well, I have to prove myself to God by being more committed, more disciplined, and more passionate about Jesus." But we've missed the point. Jesus gives us a very different message: "Say 'No' to your drivenness, your self-effort, and your compulsive desire to prove that you're worthy of Me. Instead, take up the cross. My cross has become your cross. You are in Me, and I am in You. Follow Me fully and joyfully, but because I love you so much, not to prove anything to Me or to anyone else." Rededicating ourselves in church week after week isn't the answer; it's the problem! It's the treadmill of self-effort that keeps us enslaved to performance and produces even more guilt, fear, and self-doubt.

The answer is to soak our minds and hearts in the warmth of God's grace and the truth of the gospel. When we trust Him, we find rest and peace. We can finally get off the treadmill and take His loving hand.

On the night before He was betrayed, Jesus spent a lot of time teaching His disciples some crucial truths. As He often did, Jesus used metaphors to get His points across. They may have been walking through a vineyard when He told them, "I am the vine; you are the branches. If you remain in me and I in you, you will bear much fruit; apart from me you can do nothing" (John 15:5). The life of faith, Jesus was telling them, is organic. People grow spiritually like plants grow. If they are vitally connected to the source of nourishment, they grow and bear fruit. If not, they wither away. The source of spiritual vitality isn't church attendance, Bible reading, prayer, singing, serving, or anything else we do. It's Jesus. All of our Christian activities can point us to the source of life, or they can become poor substitutes. When we engage in all those activities (or any of them) and trust them to sustain us and fill us, we'll walk away confused and empty. But if these things are means to the end of revealing the beauty and power of Christ's love, they have the effect God wants: a deeper faith, joyful obedience, and genuine fruit of changed lives—ours and others'.

In a startling statement, Jesus said, "Apart from me you can do nothing." What did He mean? Did He mean that we can't brush our teeth or tie our shoes without Him? No, He was saying that unless His grace directs us and His power works in and through us, nothing we do matters at all . . . nothing.

Paul made the same point in a famous passage in his letter to the Corinthians. The people in that church competed with each other for prestige and power. They used the activities of the church to gain leverage over others. We often read this passage at weddings, and people sigh because it's about love, but if we read it carefully, we see that Paul was sternly correcting them! He wrote that any activities that aren't empowered by the love of Jesus are completely, utterly worthless:

> If I speak in the tongues of men or of angels, but do not have love, I am only a resounding gong or a clanging cymbal. If I have the gift of prophecy and can fathom all mysteries and all knowledge, and if I have a faith that can move mountains, but do not have love, I am nothing. If I give all I possess to the poor and give over my body to hardship that I may boast, but do not have love, I gain nothing. (1 Cor. 13:1–3)

Apart from the love of God, our hard work doesn't cut it. Passion and tears have no value. Even radical sacrifice is nothing in God's sight. All our efforts that aren't tapping into the abundant source of true love and life are worth precisely nothing. They may impress others who see us work so hard, sing so passionately, and quote so much Scripture, but those things don't impress God in the least. It's time we aren't impressed with our efforts either. It's time we came to the end of ourselves.

When I realized so much of my life, especially my church life, was self-effort and self-promotion, I had a choice: to stay employed by the same slave master or retire. I chose to retire. Today, I'm still retired. My life is no longer about me; it's about Jesus. My goals are no longer self-promotion; my goals are to please the One who loves me. My strength is no longer my talents, my ability to persuade, and my capacity to get people to do what I want them to do; the unlimited power of the Spirit of God works in me and through me to fulfill God's eternal purposes.

Have you ever walked by a fruit tree and heard the apples, oranges, or peaches groan because they're straining to produce fruit? No, me either. They produce fruit naturally because their stems are connected to the branches, and all the nutrients they need flow into them. As we more fully realize we are united with Christ, one with Him, His life flows into us and produces the fruit of His character in us. Paul explained, "But the fruit of the Spirit is love, joy, peace, forbearance, kindness, goodness, faithfulness, gentleness and self-control. Against such things there is no law" (Gal. 5:22–23).

The life of Christ in us fulfills the two commandments to love God with all our hearts and love our neighbors as ourselves. Our faith in the grace of God opens the channels of His presence, power, and purposes, and the Spirit produces the life of Christ in us. As Paul points out, there's no law against that! Christianity isn't a bunch of rules and constraints; it's Jesus! It's not a sin management program; it's life and peace in the Holy Spirit!

For too long, many of us have reduced the Christian life to the things we can do for God, but we've missed the limitless love, joy and adventure of walking with our King and lover! A vibrant life of faith begins, though, with a large dose of humility. The Christian life isn't hard . . . it's impossible on our own. We simply don't have what it takes.

The Christian life isn't hard . . . it's impossible
on our own.

God's Part, Our Part

We've seen that the Holy Spirit is our Advocate. The ministry of the Spirit is expansive: He draws us to Christ initially, opens
the eyes of our hearts to understand the gospel, assures us that
we are God's children, imparts special abilities called "spiritual
gifts," enables us to grasp the meaning of Scripture, convicts us
of sin and reminds us that we're already forgiven, leads, directs,
and empowers us to bear fruit. A television commercial a few
years ago said, "If you've got it, a truck brought it." In the same
way, if we experience any spiritual life, it's the work of the Holy
Spirit. In an online post, author and pastor Tim Keller summa-
rized the Spirit's role in our lives: "The Holy Spirit's ministry is to
take truths about Jesus and make them clear to our minds and
real to our hearts—so real that they console and empower and
change us at our very center."[14]

We depend on the Holy Spirit to work in us and through
us, but we aren't passive. Paul succinctly describes our part and
God's part in our lives: "Therefore, my dear friends, as you have
always obeyed—not only in my presence, but now much more
in my absence—continue to work out your salvation with fear
and trembling, for it is God who works in you to will and to act
in order to fulfill his good purpose" (Phil. 2:12–13). The first part
of this passage sure sounds like self-effort, doesn't it? But it's
not. We don't work for our salvation by trying to do enough;
instead, the grace of God transforms us so that we gladly obey.
The "fear and trembling" isn't terror that we won't measure
up and will be cast into hell. Instead, it's the concern of a loved

child who doesn't want to do anything to displease a caring, wise, and strong parent.

The second part of the Philippians passage reminds us that every good thing comes from above, from the hand of the Father, paid for by the Son, and imparted by the Holy Spirit to us. Even our desire to love Him and our efforts to please Him ("to will and to act") comes from God.

Spiritual transformation happens from the inside out. The Pharisees did all the right things on the surface, but their hearts were far from God. They did right things but for wrong reasons. As the grace of God sinks deep into our souls, our goals, our hopes, our joys, and our concerns become the goals, hopes, joys, and concerns that are on God's heart. He becomes beautiful to us. He is our author and perfector, our Good Shepherd, our righteousness, our shield and great reward, our deliverer, our hope, our life, our wisdom, and our delight.

The change in our outlook is the work of the Spirit of God. We may do exactly the same things we'd done before, but with a different motivation. We may do less than before because we realize it was an obsessive-compulsive effort to earn approval, and we now bask in God's love. Or we may do more than before because serving our Father and King is no longer drudgery.

John Newton was the captain of a slave ship. When he became a Christian, he had a deep grasp of the limitless love, forgiveness, and acceptance of God. He also understood how our motivations are radically changed. In a beautiful and insightful hymn, he wrote:

Our pleasure and our duty,
Though opposite before,
Since we have seen His beauty
Are joined to part no more.

To see the law by Christ fulfilled
And hear His pard'ning voice,
Transforms a slave into a child,
And duty into choice.[15]

The Relational Nature of Sin

When people are performance-driven, they see sin as a list (often an arbitrary list) of rules they have to follow . . . or else. When they follow the rules, they feel superior to "those weaker, more wicked people," and when they fail to follow them, they do all kinds of gymnastics to excuse themselves, blame someone else, or feel bad enough long enough to pay for their error.

Grace-filled people have a different view of sin: It harms a cherished relationship. Sin, then, isn't just breaking some rules; it's breaking God's heart.[16] Sin is the conviction that God's way won't really satisfy us, that we know better than Him how our lives should go, and our desire for approval, power, comfort, entertainment, or things is more important than God's desire for us. Cornelius Plantinga, Jr., seminary professor at Calvin Theological Seminary, explains that sin shatters the loving, gracious, wondrous plan of God to bless us, and then through us, to bless the world. He writes about God's gracious purposes for us:

> The webbing together of God, humans, and all creation in justice, fulfillment, and delight is what the Hebrew prophets call *shalom*. In English we call it peace, but it means far more than just peace of mind or ceasefire between enemies. In the Bible, shalom means universal flourishing, wholeness, and delight—a rich state of affairs in which natural needs are justified and natural gifts fruitfully employed, a state of affairs that inspires

joyful wonder as the creator and savior opens doors and speaks welcome to the creatures in whom he delights. Shalom, in other words, is the way things are supposed to be.

Sin, then, is much more serious than transgressing archaic rules in an ancient book. Every sin is a personal rejection of a loving and wise God, the One who offers and provides shalom. Plantinga explains, "Shalom is God's designed plan for creation and redemption; sin is blamable human vandalism of these great realities and, therefore, an affront to their architect and builder."[17]

As I've spoken about God's grace, some have accused me of being "soft on sin." Quite the opposite. I believe sin is far more serious than most people believe. It's turning our backs on the One who loves us more than we can ever imagine. I have strong views about sin, but I have even stronger views on Jesus and His grace! No matter what we've done, even if we've murdered someone or if we've been the Devil's bride, the forgiveness of Jesus Christ is deeper, wider, higher, and longer than our sin. The immensity of His love is what makes sin so horrible, because sin tells Jesus, "I don't want You."

The history of God's people, Old Testament and New, is about His relentless pursuit of us and His undying desire to have a love relationship with us. The Scriptures give us many different metaphors of our relationship with God: He is our light, and He is the Bread of Life; He is the shepherd and we are His sheep; He is the potter and we are the clay. One that is often overlooked, perhaps because it is so tender and intimate, which makes us feel uneasy, is that God is our lover, and we are His beloved. The commitment, tenderness, permanence, and union we have with God can be understood as a heavenly marriage. (If the men reading this don't like being called "the bride of Christ," the women also have to handle being in the category of "sons of God" [Rev. 21:9 and Gal. 3:26–29]!)

James chastises his readers who are more enamored with success than with the Lord. If we are the bride of Christ, pursuing other lovers is spiritual adultery. "You adulterous people, don't you know that friendship with the world means enmity against God? Therefore, anyone who chooses to be a friend of the world becomes an enemy of God. Or do you think Scripture says without reason that he jealously longs for the spirit he has caused to dwell in us" (James 4:4–5)? God's jealousy isn't a sign of out-of-control anger. Not at all. Jealousy is the appropriate response of a husband or wife whose spouse is committing adultery. It's the response of a committed love. But James doesn't stop with the rebuke and warning. He assures them, "But he gives us more grace" (James 4:6).

Another passage demonstrates the underlying desires that fuel spiritual adultery. Through Jeremiah, we can hear the Lord's broken heart as He pleads with His people. God had formed a bond of love, but they considered it a yoke of slavery:

> "Long ago you broke off your yoke
> and tore off your bonds;
> you said, 'I will not serve you!'
> Indeed, on every high hill
> and under every spreading tree
> you lay down as a prostitute." (Jer. 2:20)

God compares their unrestrained, headlong pursuit of sin with a camel in heat:

> "See how you behaved in the valley;
> consider what you have done.

You are a swift she-camel
running here and there,
a wild donkey accustomed to the desert,
sniffing the wind in her craving—
in her heat who can restrain her?
Any males that pursue her need not tire themselves;
at mating time they will find her.
Do not run until your feet are bare
and your throat is dry.
But you said, 'It's no use!
I love foreign gods,
and I must go after them.'" (Jer. 2:23–25)

God uses two powerful sexual images to illustrate our passion for things that replace Him in our thoughts, desires, and pursuits. When we love the approval of people, riches, a good reputation, or pleasure more than we love God, we are like prostitutes and female camels in heat that are ravenous to be satisfied. That's spiritual adultery. We may think this term describes "those other people" because we follow rules and we're in church. Religious traditions and behaviors, when practiced to impress instead of from a heart of love for God, are another form of spiritual adultery.

In Jesus' most famous sermon, He identified two ways to give, two ways to pray, and two ways to fast. The distinction, He made it clear, isn't between "good people" and "bad people," but between those who give, pray, and fast "to be seen by men" (Matt. 6:1, 5, 16) and those who do these things purely to know, love, and serve the Father. Jesus was drawing a clear line between spiritual adultery—using spiritual activities for selfish purposes—and a grace-filled, love inspired devotion to God.

God's rebuke is always a summons to come near. For the people in Jeremiah's day, the ones who listened to Jesus, and for all of us today, God invites us back to experience the joys of knowing and loving Him. He knows (and if we pay attention, we see it, too) that those who respond to His amazing grace become "lost in wonder, love, and praise," but those (even those in our churches) who continue to try to find satisfaction in other things become filled with arrogance and shame, and they are driven and desperate. God offers us Himself, with all the joy, delight, and affection we long to experience. That's the kind of husband we have. It's a marriage made in heaven!

In His grace, God always acts in love toward us.

He's thrilled that we belong to Him.

He wants only one thing from His bride: that we would delight in His affections and eagerly receive His love.

If He asks us to carry a burden, He sweeps us off our feet and carries us.

As our husband, God never condemns, but always affirms and lovingly guides us.

He's jealous to keep our affections only on Him, because that's where we'll find true love, joy and delight.

And someday, we'll have a honeymoon that will never end!

God didn't look at our sin, shrug and say, "Well, they couldn't help it," or "It wasn't really that bad." No, Jesus looked beyond the actions to the heart that rejected Him, and instead of turning His back, He spread His arms on the cross.

All of our attempts to follow enough rules can't give us this kind of wonderful, loving relationship with God. This is what we were made for! The law was valuable in showing us our need for a Savior, and it's helpful now to show us what pleases our lover, but the law can't impart love and life; it only points us to the One who can. The law is like an abusive ex. But we've died to the power of the law (Rom. 7:1–6), and we're married to our tender, generous, patient, loving husband.

People may read these paragraphs and insist, "I go to church every week (well, almost every week), and I read my Bible and pray. I haven't killed anybody (though I wanted to a time or two). I'm not guilt of spiritual adultery!" Maybe not, but let me list a few symptoms of the condition:

- You wonder if you've done enough.

- Even worse, you live with a nagging sense of guilt because you know you haven't done enough, even though you've tried.

- You hope people have noticed your faithful actions, like church attendance or giving. (And if they haven't noticed, you tell them.)

- Your mind often drifts toward your appearance, your income, your possessions, your prestige, and your pleasure.

- You feel upset that you don't have more, and you're worried that you'll lose what you have.

- You live with secret shame over something you've done.

- You live with a sense of superiority over "those people."

- You give and serve because you're afraid not to.

- Prayer is a grind.

The law—either God's commands or the ones we make up and try to live by—makes a terrible spouse. It always demands, condemns, and asks for more. The God of grace, our true husband, lavishes His love, always forgives, and has done it all for us. The contrast couldn't be more obvious. The joy of life, genuine character change, inside-out transformation, and a life of love aren't found in following rules and trying harder when we fail. The only thing that can fill the emptiness in our hearts is to be melted by the warmth of God's unconditional (or actually, counter-conditional) love.

The more we live in grace, the more grateful we are for all God's gifts to us.

The more we live in grace, the more grateful we are for all God's gifts to us. We see all the blessings of life coming from His hand. Successes no longer make us arrogant. Accomplishments don't inflate our pride and superiority. We realize God has given us the talents, so we thank Him. God has given us the opportunities, so we're grateful. And God has blessed us abundantly, and we love Him even more.

Where the Rubber Meets the Road

In a vibrant relationship between two people—husband and wife, parent and adult child, or two close friends—there will always be some friction. We disappoint each other, we forget something that is important to the other, or we genuinely offend the person we care about. When one of these (or countless other forms of hurts) occurs, we can act like nothing happened, we can blame the other person, we can make excuses, or we can address the problem with honesty and humility. We have the same choices in our relationship with God.

"Addressing the problem with honesty and humility" is called *repentance*. It's the conversation that heals wounds, rebuilds trust, and forms even deeper bonds of love—but only if we repent in the right way. Many of us hate the very thought of repentance! When we live by rules and break them, all we feel is condemnation, and we can't stand it! We avoid repentance at all costs because it makes us feel exposed, vulnerable, and ashamed.

Actually, the Bible talks about two kinds of repentance: one that crushes and one that refreshes. After Paul wrote the letter we know as First Corinthians, it appears that he wrote a second letter. If we thought the first one was direct, the second one must have been even more pointed. We know a little of the contents of that missing letter because Paul refers to it in what we know as Second Corinthians. Obviously, he had addressed a particularly painful problem about one of the members of the church, a person who hadn't responded to earlier attempts to help him respond to God's grace with confession and restoration. However, before Paul wrote the third letter, he heard that the person had, in fact, repented. He wrote an insightful contrast of two kinds of repentance. First, he shared that true repentance always produces a kind of sorrow: "Even if I caused you sorrow by my letter, I do not regret it. Though I did regret it—I see that my letter hurt you, but only for a little while— yet now I am happy, not because you were made sorry, but because your sorrow led you to repentance. For you became sorrowful as God intended and so were not harmed in any way by us."

Then, he paints two pictures of repentance: "Godly sorrow brings repentance that leads to salvation and leaves no regret, but worldly sorrow brings death" (2 Cor. 7:8–10). Godly sorrow is a response to God's warm invitation to turn from our spiritual adultery (which is at the heart of all sin) and return to enjoy His love and forgiveness. Pastor and author Eugene Peterson explains that "the root meaning in Hebrew of *salvation* is to be broad, to become spacious, to enlarge. It carries a sense of deliverance from an existence that has become compressed, confined and cramped."[18] Godly sorrow results in freedom. The guilt and shame of sin had confined us, but in repentance, the experience of God's grace sets us free!

In contrast, "worldly sorrow"—the sense of gnawing shame that we failed to measure up, and all our attempts to do enough to overcome those awful feelings—brings death, a sense of hopelessness, alienation from God and from others, and the nagging realization that we'll do it again and feel horrible again. Who wants to repent if it only reminds us that God is angry with us? People who experience worldly sorrow may feel bad, but only because they got caught or because they suffer the consequences of their sin. They aren't sorry they've broken God's heart. Some refuse to repent because it hurts so bad, but others beat themselves bloody, calling themselves horrible names and trying to feel bad enough long enough as a kind of penance to pay for their sins. No matter how many horrible names they call themselves, no matter how long they feel ashamed, and no matter how many "good deeds" they do to try to make up for their sin, it's never enough. They always wonder if they need to do more. That's the kind of "death" Paul was talking about.

John wrote in his first letter, "If we confess our sins, he is faithful and just and will forgive us our sins and purify us from all unrighteousness" (1 John 1:9). To confess means to agree with God—about our sins and about His forgiveness. The promise is that God is "faithful and just" to forgive us. He is faithful to the covenant He has made with us that in Christ there is no longer any condemnation. And He is just to forgive us because the debt has already been fully paid. We don't need to twist God's arm, grovel in self-loathing and shame, or try to do things to make up for our sins. Our debt is completely paid, done, over, and gone! And God isn't scowling at us when we turn to Him. He longs for us to respond to His grace by experiencing the forgiveness He's already provided on the cross.

Those who believe Jesus is waiting for them with open arms *want* to repent. Those who bask in the grace of God fly *to* repentance, not *away from* it. They don't want anything to cloud the giving and receiving of love between them and God. They're glad—really glad—when the Holy Spirit taps them on the shoulder and whispers, "You know, that was selfish. That's not who you are. Remember who I've made you. It's time to make it right."

Understanding repentance transforms our motivations. Instead of being sorry we got caught and hoping God won't catch us next time, we come to our senses and ask ourselves, *Why in the world would I ever offend someone who loves me this much?*

Grace-filled believers can afford to be completely honest about their sins and flaws because their security isn't rooted in their performance.

Grace-filled believers can afford to be completely honest about their sins and flaws because their security isn't rooted in their performance. They know the love of God is strong and sure, so they can be vulnerable and open with Him . . . and with others who point out their flaws. When others have the courage to confront them, they aren't defensive, and they don't bark back to accuse the other person. They listen, ask clarifying questions, accept appropriate responsibility, and ask for forgiveness for any wrongs.

When Martin Luther nailed the 95 theses to the Wittenberg church door that launched the Protestant Reformation, the first one on the list read, "Our Lord and Master Jesus Christ . . . willed the entire life of believers to be one of repentance."[19] In spiritual life, we find a circular process that reinforces our experience of God's grace: The kindness of God leads us to repentance, honesty about our sins, and God's forgiveness takes us even deeper into His grace, which makes us even more glad to repent next time. How do we know we're living in grace every day? By our growing desire to repent and the joy and freedom it brings.

I'm sure some people read these words about "the joy of repentance" and think, *That's so far from where I've been! The thought of repenting makes me feel weak and ashamed, not loved and secure.* Yes, I know this new way of relating to God can be hard to grasp. Many of us have years of practice in the hard school of legalism and self-effort. We may feel uncomfortable with grace because it's so radical and so new to us. We find it hard, really hard, to reach out and take God's love as a free and unfettered gift. But many of us read about the marvelous grace of God and we sense His touch . . . and we long to experience more of Him.

You can be sure of this: Jesus wants you to be flooded with His love! Ask Him to touch your heart so you can taste His goodness and see the smile on His face. Admit your doubts, your fears, and your resistance, and then focus on the passages of Scripture that loudly proclaim His infinite, tender love, His brilliant and mysterious wisdom, and His ultimate power to accomplish His purposes in your life. You were made to know Him and love Him. That's where you find true fulfillment and direction . . . He's the only sure source of security, affection, and meaning.

Reframing Our Difficulties

When we go through heartaches, we may be able to identify the cause, but quite often, difficulties hit us from out of the blue. When we suffer for any reason, we may not know the cause, but we can be sure that it's *not* because God is mad and is punishing us. We may be confused about what's going on in our lives, but we don't need to be confused about the love of God. It hasn't left us, and it never will.

In Paul's last letter to the Corinthians, he told them he had endured such fierce persecution and suffering that he thought he was going to die! But Paul didn't blame God. He realized the pain was, in C. S. Lewis' famous term, "God's megaphone" to get his attention and deepen his faith. Paul told them,

> We don't want you in the dark, friends, about how hard it was when all this came down on us in Asia province. It was so bad we didn't think we were going to make it. We felt like we'd been sent to death row, that it was all over for us. As it turned out, it was the best thing that could have happened. Instead of trusting in our own strength or wits to get out of it, we were forced to trust God totally—not a bad idea since he's the God who raises the dead! And he did it, rescued us from certain doom. And he'll do it again, rescuing us as many times as we need rescuing. (2 Cor. 1:8–10, MSG)

I think many Christians actually believe in karma: If you do right, God guarantees blessings, but if you do wrong, God punishes. That's not what the Bible says about life! Certainly, we see a large measure of cause and effect related to our choices, but God isn't limited by simple answers, and He has far bigger priorities than our comfort. Sometimes, He has a different plan. We may not like the curriculum and we may not be able to pin down the cause, but heartaches and disappointments are often the classrooms where God teaches us to trust Him more. There, we realize our self-sufficiency is at an end, so we look to Him for help. Paul concluded,

> But we have this treasure in jars of clay to show that this all-surpassing power is from God and not from us. We are hard pressed on every side, but not crushed; perplexed, but not in despair; persecuted, but not abandoned; struck down, but not destroyed. We always carry around in our body the death of Jesus, so that the life of Jesus may also be revealed in our body. For we who are alive are always being given over to death for Jesus' sake, so that his life may also be revealed in our mortal body. (2 Cor. 4:7–11)

The past now has no power to condemn us, but it has great power to teach us. God never wastes a season. If we'll let Him, God will use our deepest sins and our greatest shame to drive us deeper into His grace, and when that happens, God produces a heart of compassion in us for others who feel oppressed, ashamed, broken, and helpless.

Grace changes our perspective on all kinds of suffering. When Paul endured an ongoing problem, he asked God to take it away. Instead, God explained that He had far bigger purposes for the pain Paul experienced.

> But [God] said to me, "My grace is sufficient for you, for my power is made perfect in weakness." Therefore I will boast all the more gladly about my weaknesses, so that Christ's power may rest on me. That is why, for Christ's sake, I delight in weaknesses, in insults, in hardships, in persecutions, in difficulties. For when I am weak, then I am strong. (2 Cor. 12:9–10)

Our weaknesses provide an opportunity for God to reveal His mighty power in us and through us.

I can be pretty dense. I need all these reminders of the goodness of God so I can experience Him every day, and I'll bet you do, too. If we're impressed with the God of grace, we won't be afraid of others' opinions, we won't be threatened by risks, and we won't be driven to achieve. We'll have a radically different view of our past, our successes, and our failures. We'll get off the whipsaw ride between pride and fear, and the Spirit will replace them with gratitude and humility. We'll rest, we'll delight, and we'll be more excited about honoring God than ever before.

I do not at all understand the mystery of grace—only that it meets us where we are but does not leave us where it found us.

—Anne Lamott

Consider this . . .

1. What are some ways self-effort to measure up is a form of "tyranny" and "terror"? Have you had this experience? If so, how and when?

2. When you aren't busy, what do you daydream about? What do our daydreams say about our deepest desires?

3. What are some "strongholds" in our minds? In 2 Corinthians 10:3–5, how does Paul tell us to "demolish" them? What are some practical steps we can take to demolish the strongholds in our minds?

4. Why is it important to see sin as relational instead of just breaking rules? How would you explain "spiritual adultery"?

5. Describe the two kinds of repentance. How might "godly sorrow" be something really beneficial and desirable to you?

6. Why is it important to understand that difficulties can be the most effective classroom to learn about God's grace?

7. What is God saying to you in this chapter?

7 IMPARTING GRACE

> Love cures people, both the ones who give it and the ones who receive it.
>
> **—Dr. Karl Menninger**

Jesus taught a lesson that reveals the underlying source of our attitudes, words, and actions: "No good tree bears bad fruit, nor does a bad tree bear good fruit. Each tree is recognized by its own fruit. People do not pick figs from thornbushes, or grapes from briers. A good man brings good things out of the good stored up in his heart, and an evil man brings evil things out of the evil stored up in his heart. For the mouth speaks what the heart is full of" (Luke 6:43–45).

When I was driven to perform, my heart was filled with resentment because I was trying so hard but wasn't measuring up, and I spoke in anger to the people around me. I felt the oppressive demands to do more and be more, and I made those same demands on the people closest to me. I felt out of control, so I tried to control every person and every situation, assuming control would make me feel secure. Buried deep in my heart were all kinds of fears, which surfaced in defensiveness, criticism of anyone who disagreed with me, and compulsive actions to try again and again to win the approval of others. My words were an accurate indication of the chaos, demands, open wounds, and fear that ran rampant in my heart. I hurt the people I loved, but I didn't know how to stop. The more I tried to put the clamps on my attitude and communication, the more frustrated I became and the more I pushed people away from me.

Grace revolutionized my heart, and then it revolutionized my relationships. In Jesus, I found security, kindness, patience, forgiveness, and hope. My communication with Kim and the kids, our extended family and our staff became increasingly infused with those same characteristics. These people were, in equal measures, stunned, confused, and greatly relieved!

Sudden Change

Before the revelation of the love of God captured me, Kim put up with a lot. Early in our marriage, I was driven to be successful. Failure certainly wasn't an option, but neither was mediocrity. I have no idea how many hours a week I worked, but it was a lot. I missed countless dinners and times with the kids because I was doing "important things for God." She tried reasoning with me and asked me to spend more time at home, but I didn't listen. She tried pleading with me, but I felt annoyed. Finally, after more attempts than any wife should have to try, she gave up. She concluded that my "devotion" and crammed schedule must be simply the way it has to be. We both settled in for a long season of grim determination, the twisted knife of comparison to drive me, and rampant busyness.

As the years went by, Kim occasionally again tried reasoning and pleading with me, but she knew I couldn't be persuaded. I hate to say it, but my reputation was more important than she and the children. I would never have said those words, but my actions spoke volumes.

She told a friend, "I must have tried to talk to Ben a million times, but I didn't want to sound like a nag. I was so frustrated. Each time, it initially felt good to unload on him and tell him how I felt, but I could tell that it crushed him each time. I was basically telling him that he was a failure as a husband and father, and I was breaking his heart. I didn't want to be one more voice condemning him, so most of the time, I remained quiet."

I was so driven to succeed that my work consumed every minute of every day. There was no separation between work and home. Everything revolved around my work because that's where I was getting my significance. At one point, we realized all we talked about was work, so we decided to have a moratorium on our conversations about the subject. But we had a problem: work was all that mattered, so we had nothing else to say to each other.

At some point years ago, my relationship with Kim became more like business partners. Actually, it was worse than that. I saw her as an employee whose performance would contribute to my success, or harm it. I put a lot of pressure on her to get things done, and I let her know when I thought she wasn't contributing enough. I'm afraid I treated Kim like my employee or a slave.

Thank God, my experience of the limitless love of God made a difference right away in my most cherished relationships. Kim saw it immediately: "It was shocking. I saw Ben face the same pressures, criticisms, and disappointments he'd faced countless times in the past, but his responses were so different. Instead of reacting in anger, blaming others, and demanding compliance with his wishes, he was patient. Instead of barking orders, he listened. Instead of storming off, his eyes and voice communicated love and respect. I've got to tell you, this was radical . . . and wonderful!"

When I began to rest in Jesus' love, God went to work to change me. When you live your life driven to prove yourself, you have very little time to enjoy all of God's gifts, including the people He puts in your life. When I finally believed "it is finished" and I was secure in God's grace, I began to delight in all of God's blessings, especially Kim, Kyla, and Kade. I believed I was God's treasure, so God and my family became treasures to me. I believed I was God's masterpiece, so I began to see all the beauty, intelligence, wit, and creativity in Kim and the kids. God was filling my heart, and His love overflowed into their lives. I wasn't manufacturing this love, and it wasn't some kind of phony version of the authentic thing. It was real, and they could tell.

Almost immediately, Kyla and Kade saw a difference in me. For years, I had been off limits almost all the time. When I was at home working on a message or on the phone dealing with a problem, they knew better than to bother me. And when I wasn't busy, I collapsed in exhaustion or hid from any interaction. I was spent, so I didn't have any love, time, or creativity to spend on them. It was like we were boarding in the same house, but our paths seldom crossed.

Thankfully, the changes with my kids occurred fairly quickly. Suddenly, I wasn't as driven, as preoccupied, or as exhausted. My heart was filling every day with the joy of the Lord, and I began to delight in Kyla and Kade. One of the biggest changes happened when I came home from church. In the past, I'd been a basket case on Sunday afternoons. I picked apart everything in the services, blamed myself and everyone else for any real or perceived failure, and had nothing to offer anyone physically or emotionally. Now, when I came home, I told Kim and the kids, "Hey, what do you want to do this afternoon? Let's go have some fun!" They were shocked. They wondered what kind of alien had invaded Ben Dailey's body!

Our staff noticed the same radical change. On a dime, my demeanor was completely different. For years, they had seen all the intensity in my eyes and heard it in my voice. Nothing was ever good enough for me. Now they began to see me laugh, not get ruffled by mistakes, and give them far more words of affirmation than correction—and if there was a correction, it had a completely different tone. I was no longer the judge of the Grand Inquisition; I was a friend who loved them and wanted them to thrive.

The old habits, though, didn't completely vanish. From time to time, I still felt the same old compulsions and fears, but now I had a choice. I could keep traveling down those old roads that led to exhaustion, shame, and confusion, or I could remind myself of my new identity, my union with Christ, and His delight in me. I could relax. With the right perspective, I could see every moment as an adventure with a lover instead of slavery to a harsh, condemning master.

Change—even really good change—is hard to assimilate. Even though Kim loved what God was doing in my life, she wasn't sure how to handle it. She remembers, "Ben changed so much so fast that I was almost resentful. I was so excited. This is what I'd been praying for! But he was so different that I wasn't sure how to relate to him. The new Ben wasn't the man I'd been living with. I loved what I was seeing, but I wasn't sure I could keep up. I had married a worker, not a lover. Ben was becoming a lover. It was fantastic, but very, very strange."

Learning to live in grace was like moving to a
different country with a new language and a
foreign culture.

Learning to live in grace was like moving to a different country with a new language and a foreign culture. Everything was new, awesome, and awkward. All of us had to make a lot of adjustments. We had to learn a new way of living, relating, and working.

My dominant mode to make life work had been achievement. I had given everything I had all day every day to succeed. Other people (thank the Lord) aren't just like me. They may have different tactics of winning approval, or fixing others problems to feel appreciated, or vanishing into the woodwork to avoid conflict at all costs. Apart from grace, we have to find some way to fill the hole in our hearts, carve out an identity, and protect ourselves from more hurt, but none of these strategies ultimately satisfies. Over fifteen centuries ago, Augustine identified the problem and the solution: "You have made us for yourself, O Lord, and our heart is restless until it rests in you."[20]

I had finally found rest in Jesus and all He had accomplished for me, and it changed every relationship in my life.

Tapping into the Source

Jesus and Paul often used agrarian metaphors to communicate the principles of spiritual life: vines, fruit, trees, harvest, soils, wheat, and on and on. During the Industrial Revolution, some Christian leaders began using the images of their culture as metaphors, but I think something was lost. Manufacturing and power plants may describe some aspects of the Christian experience, but they aren't organic. Flipping a switch isn't the same thing as drawing sustenance from a source of nourishment. We don't manufacture Christlike character, no matter how hard we try. It has to come from within, by the power of the Spirit, as we love Jesus and let Him pour His life into and through us to others.

Paul and John gave us three principles about the overflowing life of Christ in us. These aren't vague or complex. They are so simple a child can understand them, and yet so profound that we can never plumb the depths of them. These principles are about experiencing and expressing God's love, forgiveness, and acceptance. The concepts apply to every relationship and enable us to impart grace to the people around us.

1. Love one another. On the night Jesus was betrayed, the disciples had been with Him for over three years. They had marveled at His incredible power to heal the sick, raise the dead, feed thousands from a sack lunch, and give sight to the blind. But that wasn't all that amazed them. They were shocked that Jesus loved everyone, from the foreigners and outcasts to the rich and mighty. No one was beyond His love. Before He was arrested, Jesus gave final instructions to His followers. At one point that night, He told them, "A new command I give you: Love one another. As I have loved you, so you must love one another. By this everyone will know that you are my disciples, if you love one another" (John 13:34–35).

They must have been stunned. They probably thought, *Love like He loves? You've got to be kidding! That's impossible!*

Yes, it's totally impossible, unless we find a new source of love and power. The gospel is that source. After the crucifixion and the resurrection and on the day of Pentecost, the disciples were cleansed of sin and empowered to love even those who persecuted them. That's supernatural!

Some people are really hard to love. They get under our skin, do things to hurt us, or exasperate us in countless ways. We don't want to love them. We want to avoid them or blast them!

Where do we find the ability to love the unlovable? From knowing that Jesus loved us when we were unlovable. He demonstrated the depth of His love by "loving us to the end"— His death on the cross. When our hearts are overwhelmed with His unconditional love, we'll be able to love annoying people, dull people, threatening people, demanding people, big people, little people, and everyone else. It's not something we can generate on our own. God has to make His love so real to our hearts that it can't be contained!

2. Forgive one another. Forgiveness is at the heart of the Christian faith, but many believers live with unresolved hurt and anger, which soon turn into bitterness. We're wounded, we feel betrayed, and the people don't even care that they've hurt us. Still, God has called us to forgive, and even to go further, to love our enemies. Where can we find the strength to do that? By looking at the cross.

The apostle Paul put the pieces of the puzzle together in his letter to the Ephesians: "Get rid of all bitterness, rage and anger, brawling and slander, along with every form of malice. Be kind and compassionate to one another, forgiving each other, just as in Christ God forgave you" (Eph. 4:31–32). We can't give away something we don't possess. To forgive those who have hurt us, we have to be amazed at the fact that God has forgiven us. We don't excuse them, we don't minimize the pain, and we don't deny that the wound actually happened. Those are the most common ways people (even Christians) try to "get over" the pain of being deeply hurt, but these strategies eventually backfire, leaving more hurt, confusion and resentment.

When we don't forgive, we secretly (or not so secretly) long for revenge. In an article for *Christianity Today*, author and pastor Lewis Smedes observed, "Vengeance is having a videotape planted in your soul that cannot be turned off. It plays the painful scene over and over again inside your mind. . . . And each time it plays you feel the clap of pain again. . . . Forgiving turns off the videotape of pained memory. Forgiving sets you free."[21]

Some of us protest, "But I'd never treat anyone the way that person treated me. It's not fair that I have to forgive!" No, we might not sin in exactly the same way the person sinned in hurting us, but we've committed our own sins that required the death of the Son of God to forgive. We may not have committed the same sin as the one who abused or abandoned us, but we still needed the full measure of Christ's sacrifice. When we're convinced that our sins required Jesus to die, we'll be thrilled that we're forgiven, and we'll have the power and resources to forgive those who have hurt us.

3. Accept one another. We smile, we nod, we speak nice things to people in their presence, but we cut them to shreds behind their backs. Or we may avoid them. We feel superior to "those people." Most of us have an unspoken set of categories: acceptable, tolerable, and unacceptable. We reserve our warmth only for people in the first group.

When we read the Gospels, we find that Jesus had only one category: acceptable. No one was outside His orbit; no one was excluded from His affection. The scandal of His life was that He welcomed the people others deemed unacceptable . . . and fully embraced them. He hung out with despised prostitutes, Mafioso tax collectors, the sick, foreigners, women, children, lepers, and others the religious elite considered unclean.

Near the end of Paul's most exhaustive letter about the glories of grace, he explained that the acceptance we've received in Christ spills over to every relationship. He wrote,

> May the God who gives endurance and encouragement give you the same attitude of mind toward each other that Christ Jesus had, so that with one mind and one voice you may glorify the God and Father of our Lord Jesus Christ. Accept one another, then, just as Christ accepted you, in order to bring praise to God. (Rom. 15:5–7)

It's easy for us to put particular people in the "tolerable" and "unacceptable" categories. Where do we find the warmth, the love, and the motivation to accept them as friends, brothers, and sisters? We have to go deeper into the limitless grace of God. We were outcasts, enemies of God, with nothing to offer Him in the least. But in our ugliness of sin, Jesus paid the price to draw us close. He doesn't just tolerate us. We were adopted as children of the Father! When that glorious fact saturates our hearts, we can move toward those we have ignored, reach out to the ones we've despised, and love those we used to consider unacceptable.

Loving people with the love of God, though, isn't always easy and pleasant. We sometimes need to speak the hard truth to give people an opportunity to change their mind and direction. Paul called the Galatians "foolish," and Jesus called the Pharisees "whitewashed tombs," a "brood of vipers," and children of the Devil! Were these labels designed to crush people? No, Paul and Jesus wanted them to wake up, to see how far they had fallen from the grace and purposes of God. In the same way, it's not love to let an addict, a liar, a prodigal, an abuser, or a thief get away with sin again and again. If we love

them, we'll say the hard things to them and give them opportunities to change the direction of their lives. If we've first forgiven
them, our words and actions won't be energized by revenge,
but from a sincere desire for what's best for them. Loving people
this way is one of the most challenging things we will ever do.
It requires us to depend on God for wisdom and courage . . .
maybe more than we ever have before.

Loving people this way is one of the most
challenging things we will ever do.

Family Mode

For many years, I lived in "factory mode," cranking out
products, focusing on growth, afraid of the people I considered
shareholders, and marketing myself so people would buy what
I was selling—and always talking about God in the process! No
matter how well things went, it was never enough. I lived under
the constant pressure to grow faster.

When God touched my heart with His grace, I had to reeval-
uate everything: my methods and my motives. My life was no
longer about performance; it was about the life of Christ in
me and now working through me to touch others. Instead of
factory mode, I got into family mode. I'm a child of God, one He
delights to call His own, and He has invited me to work along-
side Him in the family enterprise of spreading His grace to every
part of our community and every corner of the world.

As I began reading the Bible with fresh eyes, I realized the
story of God begins in a garden, the garden of Eden, and it ends
in a garden, the new heaven and new earth. In both gardens,
people enjoy the presence of God. They work, but not to earn

points with God, only to honor Him and advance His glory. Of course, we live in between those two gardens, but even now, God offers a vast measure of peace, rest, beauty, joy, and a different reason to work—but only if we let the grace of God sink deep into our hearts.

If we choose to live as the family of God in the garden of His delights, we can leave the smog and grind of factory life behind. We still work, and we may work harder than ever before, but for a far different purpose. Actually, lovers outwork laborers, and loved children work smarter than slaves. Kim, Kyla, Kade, and our staff at the church were no longer a reflection of my identity, so their good behavior no longer bolstered my reputation, and their failures no longer tarnished it. I was free to love them and seek the best for them!

When I think back on the way I treated the kids before my grace awakening, I cringe. If we were in a public place, like a restaurant, and one of them did something that wasn't perfect behavior, I barked, "Don't do that! It's embarrassing to your mother and me!" Even worse, sometimes I twisted the knife by glaring at them, "If you embarrass us, we'll embarrass you." I was threatening my own children . . . for being children. The way I treated them produced fear we could see as they cowered whenever they failed, and it also probably produced a large measure of resentment under the surface.

God never is threatened by our behavior, and He doesn't threaten us. He may say, "Your behavior makes Me sad. I have much more for you than this," but He immediately assures us, "but I love you and I've forgiven you."

I was so glad to confess my sin of self-absorbed anger and attempts to control people. I apologized to Kim, our children, and our staff, spelling out the damage I'd done, with no excuses. I asked them to forgive me, and they were gracious to me. I explained that I had a long, long way to go to learn to live in grace. At hundreds of points, I was able to identify my old controlling, condemning behavior. I felt deep pangs of godly sorrow, and now, a new flood of God's forgiveness. I often told the people closest to me, "I know I used to react in anger and demands when situations like this happened, and I'm so sorry. God is working in me to change me. Please be patient with me." I asked them to help me by praying for me, encouraging me, and telling me when they felt I was reverting to the old Ben. Spiritual growth is a team sport, and I need all the help I can get!

With my family, my friends, our church staff, and everyone else in my life, I want to give and receive plenty of encouragement. The stakes are too high to be a loner. The writer of Hebrews tells us, "But encourage one another daily, as long as it is called 'Today,' so that none of you may be hardened by sin's deceitfulness" (Heb. 3:13). "Sin's deceitfulness" isn't just immorality, stealing, and murder; in my life it has looked like self-righteousness, self-defensiveness, and self-justification. I need people to remind me every day not to drift back into those old, painful, destructive patterns—and to remind me that I'm a new person, with a new identity, a new purpose, a new power, and new source of love. You need the same reminders.

I rearranged my schedule because my priorities changed. Before, I worked eighty to ninety hours a week, and even when I wasn't officially working, my mind couldn't stop thinking about all that needed to happen "at the factory" to produce more. I began to relax, to love people instead of using them, and to genuinely enjoy spending time with them. Kim and the children had to adjust to the new Ben Dailey, and my staff wondered if it would last.

The grace of God gave me an increasing ability to be more like the father in Jesus' story of the two sons. When I encountered younger brothers who were messing up their lives, I didn't point out all their sins. I just assured them of the Father's love and forgiveness, and I welcomed them home. And when I faced the self-righteousness and resentment of elder brothers, I pleaded with them to come to the feast of God's goodness, mercy, and love. I certainly didn't blast them for being so slow to grasp grace . . . I'd been just like them not long before!

Repairing the damage caused by legalism and demands takes time. People we've hurt may feel relieved that we're no longer biting their heads off, passive-aggressively talking behind their backs, or spinning facts to create our own version of reality, but they may not trust us for a while. And sometimes, we've created an open wound that's hard to heal.

A friend of mine was a driven CEO of a mid-sized corporation, and he treated his family much like I'd treated mine, as an extension of his identity and reputation. His teenage son complied meekly for years, but when he turned sixteen, he'd had enough. He rebelled in every way he could, running as far away from his dad as he could and hanging out with a rough crowd. At one point, he was arrested. He dreaded calling his dad, but he made the call.

For months, the father had been learning about grace, and God was changing his life. He had tried to talk to his son about his new experiences of God's love, but the young man didn't buy it. Now, on the way home from jail, the father and son had an opportunity to begin again. The dad cancelled an important business trip so he could spend time with his son. Instead of blasting the boy for being irresponsible and bringing shame on the family, the dad assured him of his love, and told him that he was completely forgiven. To the boy's utter shock, the dad apologized for being so preoccupied with work and not being there for him. The boy had been arrested, but the dad asked for forgiveness! It was the beginning of a wonderful restoration in the relationship.

In the weeks and months that followed, the son's fury toward his dad gradually subsided, and in fact, he became his father's chief supporter. The father was trying to be a grace-filled CEO and change the culture of his office environment, but many of his top staff resisted the change. They were used to the power plays and manipulation, and they didn't know how to treat people with truth and respect. Many of them opposed the dad, and some of them left the company. Through all the transitions in the corporate office, the dad talked to his son, asked for his advice, and received plenty of support. The two had been bitter adversaries, but they became trusted allies. Two years later, the son announced that he wanted to get a business degree so he could work in the company with his father. Grace worked a miracle of redemption, reconciliation, and restoration.

Beyond Our Walls

When we experience the overwhelming love of God, we can't stop talking about it. Like a scientist who has just discovered the cure for cancer, we want everyone to know the answer to the deepest problem of life! When we're excited about grace, we don't look down on any race, class, or segment of people in society. Like Jesus, we love them all. In our country, however, Christians are having the opposite impact. In 1996 and 2009, George Barna conducted surveys of Americans who had no religious affiliation. In the first one, 85 percent viewed Christianity as a positive influence, but thirteen years later only 16 percent had a favorable view of Christianity—and just 3 percent had a favorable view of evangelicals.[22] The people of God are failing to communicate the love of God to a needy world.

> Attempts to live by performance always lead
> to comparison, competition, and judgment—
> and the losers are always excluded.

Attempts to live by performance always lead to comparison, competition, and judgment—and the losers are always excluded. In Jesus' day, the Pharisees looked down on all those who were not as moral, as dedicated to the Bible, and as devoted to traditions as they were. They despised prostitutes, tax collectors, and Samaritans; they overlooked women and children as though they weren't even there; and they believed poverty and sickness were the results of moral failures. In other words, the only people they valued were the ones they saw when they looked at each other.

Today, what do the masses of people see when they look at Christians? I'm afraid they see people who are *against* almost everything and *for* very little, who are always right, who are quick to condemn and slow to love. That's not true in all cases, of course. God's people have given generously and served sacrificially in many communities in countless ways, but the Barna surveys show that the people of our country too often see something very unattractive—very unlike Jesus—when they look at Christians.

I'm not suggesting we lower our standards or water down the truth. Jesus did neither. Instead, He loved. He really loved. His obvious affection for people attracted the outsiders and infuriated the insiders. My guess is that His love, if genuinely expressed, still has the same effect today.

In *Vanishing Grace*, Philip Yancey tells a story about a meeting with Henri Nouwen, one of the most influential believers in the last century. The two men discussed the story of Jesus meeting the Samaritan woman at the well. Nouwen had just returned from San Francisco, where he had visited patients in an AIDS clinic. He realized the men and women in the clinic were much like the Samaritan woman: despised, feared, and alone due to the choices they had made.

Nouwen explained to Yancey that as he spent time listening to the stories of the patients, his prayers changed. Among the accounts of addiction and promiscuity, he heard the unmistakable sounds of thirst for a love that had never been quenched—just as the Samaritan woman was still looking for love when Jesus spoke to her that day. Nouwen learned to pray, "God, help me to see others not as my enemies or as ungodly but rather as *thirsty* people. And give me the courage and compassion to offer your Living Water, which alone quenches deep thirst."

Henri Nouwen went where thirsty people gathered. There, he found broken-down sinners, people who had ruined their lives through destructive choices. But he didn't condemn; he listened to them tell their stories. In listening, hearts connected, and these people became more than stereotypes, caricatures, and statistics. They became men and women who were thirsty for God's love.[23]

And that's our prayer also. God, give us grace to see the people in our neighborhoods, our schools, our companies, our country, and around the world as those who are thirsty. Give us enough love for them so we'll slow down and listen to their hearts, and then use us to connect them to the source of life-giving water.

A New Way to Live

Years ago, I came to the conclusion that life was a grind, and it would always be a grind. I heard (and said) all kinds of statements meant to sound heroic but reinforced the grind of self-effort and demands: "Only the tired accomplish anything important," "When the going gets tough, the tough get going," and "Suck it up one more time." If anyone had tried to tell me that Jesus offers peace, joy, and delight, I would have laughed and walked away.

Then I realized—and experienced—a revolutionary truth: "It is for freedom that Christ has set us free. Stand firm, then, and do not let yourselves be burdened again by a yoke of slavery" (Gal. 5:1). I had lived under the cruel, oppressive yoke of slavery to performance. I thought it was all God offered. Grace, I assumed, was only for unbelievers to become believers. The most monumental realization of my life was that I was wrong! God's magnificent grace is for me. I can live and breathe in the warmth of His love and the power of His Spirit. His life *is* my life.

I now have a different message: Embrace Jesus, and know that you are His treasure. You are more valuable to Him than all the stars in the sky. All of His love and life, His power and wisdom, are in you because you are in Him. Do you long to be loved? On the cross He has demonstrated the enormity of His love for you. Do you want to be valued? He stepped out of heaven because you mean more to Him than all the riches of glory. Do you want your life to count? He invites you to be His partner in the greatest adventure the world has ever known.

Do you want to make a difference? Great! Do it, but not to earn points with God or to impress people. Serve and give out of a heart overflowing with delight in the love of God. The Lord isn't looking for slaves to command; He wants sons and daughters who are so thrilled to be His that they can't stop talking about Him. We love others—and serve them without pretence or manipulation—only when our hearts are first filled with the love of God (1 John 4:19).

God's grace is limitless.

Don't let fear and doubt cloud your heart any longer. God's grace is limitless. You can't be any more forgiven, you can't be any more loved, and you can't be any more accepted than you are right now in Jesus Christ. Like the prostitute who poured out the ointment on Jesus and wiped His feet with her tears, go to Jesus. Experience the warmth of His love, and then pour out your affection for the One who loves you. Hold nothing back. Enjoy all the gifts God has lavished on you. When you feel yourself slipping back into self-effort and the desire to impress others by your performance, run back to grace! When your prayers aren't answered the way you hoped, realize that God always gives us what we would have asked for if we knew what He knows. Our Father knows best. We can enjoy Him, and we can trust Him.

Two passages from the Old Testament describe our predicament and God's gracious solution. Song of Songs is a beautiful picture of love between a man and his bride, but for centuries, scholars and preachers have seen this relationship as a metaphor of our connection with God. The opening verses describe the bride's affection: "Let him kiss me with the kisses of his mouth—for your love is more delightful than wine. Pleasing is the fragrance of your perfumes; your name is like perfume poured out" (Song 1:2–3). When we have even a glimpse into the wonder of grace, God's love is more delightful than anything we ever imagined!

But like most of us, the bride suffers from an identity crisis. She's convinced she's not worthy of her lover's affection. She looks in the mirror and sees that she's "dark," rejected by her family, and forced to labor in the hot sun in a vineyard, but in her hard work, she neglected her own vineyard (Song 1:5–7). Like her, many of us have labored hard to prove ourselves, appease demanding people, or earn God's approval, but we've neglected our own vineyards—a deep, rich, life-giving experience of the grace of God. The groom saw his bride as breathtakingly beautiful, but she had difficulty experiencing his tender and passionate love. Can you identify with her? I sure can. I lived that way for years.

Many Christians today are exhausted from self-effort, prideful they're not like "those people" who don't follow God's rules, or ashamed that they can't ever measure up. They're laboring in the wrong vineyard! Thankfully, God hasn't left us there. He gently and persistently calls our names and invites us to come back. Through the prophet Hosea, God whispers and shouts:

> "Therefore I am now going to allure her;
> I will lead her into the wilderness
> and speak tenderly to her.
> There I will give her back her vineyards,
> and will make the Valley of Achor a door of hope.
> There she will respond as in the days of her youth,
> as in the day she came up out of Egypt."
> (Hos. 2:14–15)

The Valley of Achor was a place where God's people experienced a curse, but God turned it into a source of hope. In the same way, all the commands of God showed us that we can't earn a good record with Him. While we continue to try so hard, we live under a curse. But the law isn't evil or wrong; it's our tutor, our teacher, and our guide to point us to the Savior, our true source of hope. As we soak in His unmerited but unlimited grace, God gives us a new vineyard, one that is a source of nourishment, joy, gratitude, and purpose. Under the law, God appeared to be a demanding taskmaster, but under grace, He is a compassionate, attentive, generous husband who delights in us and showers us with rapturous love (Hos. 2:16).

We have a choice. We can keep sweating, striving, and grinding in a rocky vineyard that never satisfies, or we can listen to the gentle voice of our lover and enjoy His affection.

The grace of God wasn't our idea. We didn't manufacture the concept, and we didn't initiate a relationship with God. First to last, God pursues us. He pursues us, captures our hearts, and brings us into the kingdom, and He is the One who "opens the eyes of our hearts" by His Spirit to convince us of His affection, kindness, and purpose. Some of us are a little slow to respond to His initiative, but that's okay. He's incredibly patient. I'm just glad I finally woke up. I'm thrilled that God has convinced me of His limitless love. No matter how long it took, it's worth it.

My prayer is that you will be amazed at the limitless love of God. It's the life you were meant to live.

There is no substitute for the comfort supplied by the utterly taken-for-granted relationship.

—Iris Murdoch

Consider this . . .

1. When we don't live in grace, what do we want, need, and demand from the people closest to us? How do they feel when we treat them this way?

2. What are some specific ways grace can revolutionize relationships—even yours?

3. Who are some individuals or groups others often put in the "tolerate" or "unacceptable" categories? Who are the people in these categories in your life?

4. What does it (or might it) look like to love, forgive, and accept these people by experiencing God's limitless love, forgiveness, and acceptance?

5. How would you describe the differences between "factory mode" and "family mode"?

6. What can we expect in our relationships when God begins to change us so that His grace transforms our hearts, our attitudes, and our words?

7. What is God saying to you in this chapter?

ENDNOTES

1. Brent Curtis and John Eldredge, *The Sacred Romance,* (Nashville: Thomas Nelson, 1997), 4.

2. Tim Keller, *The Prodigal God* (Dutton: New York, 2008), 70–71.

3. Cavan Sleczkowski, "Homeless Heir to $300 Million Huguette Clark Fortune Found Dead," *The Huffington Post*, December 31, 2012, www.huffingtonpost. com/2012/12/31/homeless-heir-found-dead-300-million-huguette-clark-fortune-found_n_2388339.html

4. Miroslav Volf, *Free of Charge* (Grand Rapids: Zondervan, 2005), 24, 132.

5. Robert Farrar Capon, *The Parables of Grace* (Grand Rapids: Eerdmans, 1988), 126.

6. Larry Crabb, *Finding God* (Grand Rapids: Zondervan, 1993), 18.

7. J. I. Packer, *Knowing God* (Downers Grove: InterVarsity Press, 1973), 196.

8. Thomas Chalmers, "The Expulsive Power of a New Affection," cited at: www.christianity.com/Christian%20 Foundations/The%20Essentials/11627257/

9. Dr. James Richards, *Grace: The Power to Change* (New Kensington, PA: Whitaker House, 1993), 172.

10. I originally read these questions on the blog of writer and speaker Paul Ellis: "Your Glorious New Past," August 3, 2011, escapetoreality.org/2011/08/03/your-glorious-new-past. The questions stimulated the content of this section of the chapter.

11. World Health Organization, www.who.int/nmh/publications/ncd_report_full_en.pdf

12. "The Impact of Stress," American Psychological Association, www.apa.org/news/press/releases/stress/2011/impact.aspx

13. Martin Luther, *Commentary on Galatians*, (Objective Systems, 2006), 2:14.

14. From a Facebook post, www.facebook.com/TimKellerNYC/posts/596676613705562

15. John Newton, "Love Constraining to Obedience," *The Works of the Rev. John Newton*, 624.

16. From a sermon by Tim Keller, "The True Bridegroom," Redeemer Presbyterian Church, audio: sermons2.redeemer.com/sermons/true-bridegroom.

17. Cornelius Plantinga, Jr., "Sin: Not the Way It's Supposed to Be," tgc-documents.s3.amazonaws.com/cci/Pantinga.pdf.

18. Eugene Peterson, *Reversed Thunder: The Revelation of John and the Praying Imagination* (New York: HarperSanFrancisco, 1991), 153.

19. Martin Luther, "Disputation of Doctor Martin Luther on the Power and Efficacy of Indulgences" (1517), Thesis 1.

20. St. Augustine, *The Confessions*, trans. Henry Chadwick (New York: Oxford University Press, 1991), 3.

21. Lewis Smedes, "Forgiveness: The Power To Change The Past," *Christianity Today*, January 7, 1983.

22. Cited in David Kinnaman and Gabe Lyons, *UnChristian: What a New Generation Really Thinks about Christianity . . . and Why It Matters* (Grand Rapids: Baker, 2007), 24–25.

23. Philip Yancey, *Vanishing Grace* (Grand Rapids: Zondervan, 2014), 28).

USING *LIMITLESS* IN CLASSES AND GROUPS

This book is designed for individual study, small groups, and classes. The best way to absorb and apply these principles is for each person to study and answer the questions at the end of each chapter then to discuss them in either a class or a group environment.

Each chapter's questions are designed to promote reflection, application, and discussion. Order enough copies of the book for everyone to have a copy. For couples, encourage both to have their own book so they can record their individual reflections.

A recommended schedule for a small group or class might be:

Week 1

Introduce the material. As a group leader, tell your story, share your hopes for the group, and provide books for each person. Encourage people to read the assigned chapter each week and answer the questions.

Weeks 2–8

Each week, introduce the topic for the week and share a story of how God has used the principles in your life. In small groups, lead people through a discussion of the questions at the end of the chapter. In classes, teach the principles in each chapter, use personal illustrations, and invite discussion. Week 2 will cover the introduction and chapter 1.

Personalize Each Lesson

Don't feel pressured to cover every question in your group discussions. Pick out three or four that had the biggest impact on you, and focus on those, or ask people in the group to share their responses to the questions that meant the most to them that week.

Make sure you personalize the principles and applications. At least once in each group meeting, add your own story to illustrate a particular point.

Make the Scriptures come alive. Far too often, we read the Bible like it's a phone book, with little or no emotion. Paint a vivid picture for people. Provide insights about the context of people's encounters with God, and help people in your class or group sense the emotions of specific people in each scene.

Focus on Application

The questions at the end of each chapter and your encouragement to group members to be authentic will help your group take big steps to apply the principles they're learning. Share how you are applying the principles in particular chapters each week, and encourage them to take steps of growth, too.

Three Types of Questions

If you have led groups for a few years, you already understand the importance of using open questions to stimulate discussion. Three types of questions are *limiting, leading,* and *open*. Many of the questions at the end of each day's lesson are open questions.

Limiting questions focus on an obvious answer, such as, "What does Jesus call himself in John 10:11?" These don't stimulate reflection or discussion. If you want to use questions like this, follow them with thought-provoking, open questions.

Leading questions require the listener to guess what the leader has in mind, such as, "Why did Jesus use the metaphor of a shepherd in John 10?" (He was probably alluding to a passage in Ezekiel, but many people don't know that.) The teacher who asks a leading question has a definite answer in mind. Instead of asking this kind of question, you should just teach the point and perhaps ask an open question about the point you have made.

Open questions usually don't have right or wrong answers. They stimulate thinking, and they are far less threatening because the person answering doesn't risk ridicule for being wrong. These questions often begin with "Why do you think . . .?" or "What are some reasons that . . .?" or "How would you have felt in that situation?"

Preparation

As you prepare to teach this material in a group or class, consider these steps:

Carefully and thoughtfully read the book. Make notes, highlight key sections, quotes, or stories, and complete the reflection section at the end of each day's chapter. This will familiarize you with the entire scope of the content.

As you prepare for each week's class or group, read the corresponding chapter again and make additional notes.

Tailor the amount of content to the time allotted. You won't have time to cover all the questions, so pick the ones that are most pertinent.

Add your own stories to personalize the message and add impact.

Before and during your preparation, ask God to give you wisdom, clarity, and power. Trust Him to use your group to change people's lives.

Most people will get far more out of the group if they read the chapter and complete the reflection each week. Order books before the group or class begins or after the first week.

ABOUT THE AUTHOR

Ben Dailey serves as the lead pastor of Calvary Church, a multi-site church in the Dallas/Fort Worth Metroplex. He is the author of *Collide: When Your Desires Meet God's Heart.* Known for his creative style of communication and passion for non-conventional ministry, he reaches one of the most culturally diverse congregations in the nation. His unique ministry approach, along with his passion to reach the unchurched, has produced an atmosphere for record growth. Ben has served as a church planter and ministry consultant.

Ben grew up on the coast of central California. After graduating from high school, he planned to go to college in Los Angeles. He was excited about the bright lights, beautiful people, and fast living . . . but God had other plans. Late one night, God met him and turned him around. In an instant, God charted a new direction for Ben's life.

Ben's character, passions, values, and ministry philosophy have been shaped by the powerful influence of two men: his father and Don George. Ben's dad has been a consistent model of joyful sacrifice. Ben always remembers his parents' home being a place of refuge to people in need. Reaching out to the disadvantaged was normal in their family. But for Ben's dad, it was never merely duty. He delighted in caring for those who were overlooked by society.

Early in Ben's ministry, he met Don George , senior pastor at Calvary Church in Irving, Texas. Ben didn't know it at the time, but God had put it in Don's heart to bring Ben and Kim under his care. Ben became his assistant, and Pastor George mentored him in every aspect of pastoral ministry. Ben saw him in every conceivable situation in serving God, church members, the community, and pastors of other churches. Pastor George's influence profoundly shaped Ben's heart and his career.

After Ben served as a pastor for several years in another city, Don George asked him to pray about coming back to Calvary Church. In the years since his return, Ben has become the lead pastor and has led the church to reach out far beyond its then-existing membership. The church has become known for ethnic diversity, wide-ranging ministries to the poor, and powerful outreach to the lost. In these years, the church has seen phenomenal growth.

Ben has been married to his wife, Kim, for twenty-one years. They have two children, Kyla and Kade.

FOR MORE INFORMATION

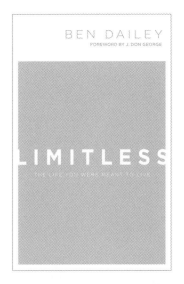

For more information about these and other helpful resources, visit **www.myhealthychurch.com**

It's inevitable. Sooner or later, our desires will collide with God's heart. His purposes are far higher than ours, His wisdom far deeper, and His love far wider. From our limited perspective, we think we know what God should do to bless our lives. We have dreams for our careers, our marriage, our kids, and every other aspect of life. Sometimes, we're right on track, but today, tomorrow, or a year from now, we'll realize our hopes and dreams have crashed. At that moment, we have a decision to make: Will we shake our fist at God, walk away, or cling to Him more than ever before? The moment our desires collide with God may seem like the end of a dream, but in reality, it's the beginning of fresh insights and renewed hope.